JOHN C. LAMBERT

FIRE
&
ICE

**MISSIONARY ADVENTURES
OF THE 1800s**

Fire & Ice: Missionary Adventures of the 1800s

an adaptation of John C. Lambert's *The Romance of Missionary Heroism: True Stories of the Intrepid Bravery and Stirring Adventures of Missionaries With Uncivilized Man, Wild Beasts, and the Forces of Nature in All Parts of the World*

The Romance of Missionary Heroism was originally published by Seeley & Co. in 1907 and has been edited and abridged by Pioneers-USA in 2021. Illustrations reproduced from original publication are in the public domain.

© 2021, Pioneers-USA

Cover design: Eric Powell
Editorial: Maxine McDonald, Marti Wade, Cadi Murphy

ISBN: 978-0-9899545-9-4

Pioneers mobilizes teams to glorify God among unreached peoples by initiating church-planting movements in partnership with local churches. For more information on Pioneers, visit *Pioneers.org.*

CONTENTS

CONTENTS

FOREWORD

Two British statesmen and a Spanish-American philosopher are all credited with some variation of the saying, "Those who forget history are doomed to repeat it." A more optimistic corollary is that those who remember history have an opportunity to repeat the best parts of it. The history of the worldwide proclamation of the gospel is worth both remembering and repeating.

The Church has advanced for two thousand years through a mosaic of thousands of individual stories. This book invites you to pause and consider a few of them. You'll find tales of adventure from the swamps of Guyana to isolated settlements of the Arctic as God's people pursued His great redemption program for the nations. What value system motivated these ordinary members of the body of Christ to choose a life of extreme risk, sacrifice, tragedy and adventure? To most people, it probably seemed like they had lost their minds, but they never lost heart. They persevered at great personal cost for the sake of great spiritual reward.

The people you admire reveal a lot about your values. Who are your heroes? Whose stories do you hold up as examples to the next generation? Are they scientists? Athletes? Entrepreneurs? Or are they people who plunged headlong into the current of redemptive history and let it carry them to the uttermost parts of the world?

Every single member of the body of Christ is a product of missionary stories like the ones told in this book. The spiritual heritage of every believer, without exception, connects back to a missionary effort of some kind. We stand in a long line of succession from the saints of old. And not just the biblical characters that we all appreciate and seek to emulate, but also the generations of countless heroes who have lived and served between the time of the apostles and the present day. This book tells the stories of one subset of those faithful servants of the gospel—those who dedicated their lives to cross-cultural ministry.

I invite you to step away from the busyness for a few hours to consider the kind of life that is truly worth living, the kind of life God is calling all the people of His kingdom to pursue. Jesus said to His disciples, "Others have done the hard work, and you have reaped the benefits of their labor" (John 4). These are the stories of people who did the hard work, not in search of riches or fame, but purely to see the name of Jesus exalted where it had never been heard.

Jesus also said that in His kingdom, "The last will be first and the first will be last" (Matthew 20:16). Other passages indicate many people are going to be surprised when we find out, in the final analysis, who really is great. I'm convinced the characters in this book are some of God's most honored servants. None of them recognized themselves as being great or sought greatness in their own or the world's eyes. They attained greatness as they obeyed and glorified God among all the peoples He created. May we imitate these heroes and deliberately repeat their history of faithfulness to our great God.

Steve Richardson
President, Pioneers-USA
Orlando, 2021

INTRODUCTION

THIS BOOK IS AN ABBREVIATED and updated version of the 1907 anthology *The Romance of Missionary Heroism* by John C. Lambert. A Scottish minister and a contemporary of many of the missionary pioneers he wrote about, Lambert believed that the "adventurous and stirring side of missionary experience needs to be brought out, and emphasis laid upon the fact that the romantic days of missions are by no means past."[1] That is as true today as it was in 1907.

The missionary task remains essentially the same from century to century. The pioneers who played dramatic roles in reaching the world in the 1800s may at first seem rather old fashioned and out of touch with modern life, but if you strip away the outdated vocabulary and technology, their stories begin to feel remarkably fresh and relevant. Like present-day missionaries, 19th century heroes struggled with language study, missed their families, craved familiar food, were disrupted by political turmoil, used business to access unreached communities, partnered with local believers, debated whether to flee or face danger and sought to bring the unchanging message of the gospel to people who had no other way of hearing it.

Through these stories, present-day believers glimpse the lives of pioneer missionaries and local Christians in locations ranging from the Arctic Circle to just beyond the southern tip of Patagonia, from the coral islands of Fiji to the Himalayan plateau of Tibet. And the diversity of people God called and equipped to carry out His worldwide mission in the 1800s is just as staggering as the variety of places He sent them.

Fire & Ice traces common threads in a dozen separate tales of adventure and redemption, told in sets of two. Characters as

---

1. From Lambert's introduction to *The Romance of Missionary Heroism*.

different from one another as Annie Taylor (a British woman considered "delicate" in her time), Joseph Neesima (a runaway samurai) and Saccibarra (a Guyanese sorcerer) shared much in common, not just in faith, but also in practice. Kapi'olani, a Hawaiian chief, climbed a volcano to prove the power of her God. George Mackay, a Canadian with Scottish Highland roots, pulled teeth in Taiwan to prove the exact same thing. Coley Patteson, grandnephew of the poet Coleridge, and Allen Gardiner, a former navy captain, died on two beaches 7,500 miles apart for exactly the same reason: they believed that the gospel of Jesus Christ is for every person on earth.

Missions looks somewhat different now than it did in the 1800s, but the essential task of spiritual transformation remains the same and the accompanying drama and adventure continue unabated. Missionaries today encounter fewer practicing cannibals than when Lambert wrote, but some of them still work in places where snakes grow big enough to eat adult humans on at least an occasional basis.

For this adaptation of Lambert's book, we have selected stories that highlight the creativity, faithfulness and determination of our missionary forerunners. We updated some of the language and condensed the content for an easier read while seeking to maintain the original voice and emphasis. Lambert's hope was that "some of those into whose hands this book may come will be induced by what they read to make fuller acquaintance with the lives and aims of our missionary heroes, and so will catch something of that spirit which led them to face innumerable dangers, toils, and trials among heathen and often savage peoples, whether in the frozen North or the burning South, whether in the hidden depths of some vast continent or among the scattered 'islands of the ocean seas.'"[2]

You won't find any perfect models to emulate in this book, but you might find faith that convicts, courage that inspires and adventures that excite you to strike out with boldness and humility on a similar path of missionary intention. If you do, you'll find

---

2. From Lambert's introduction to *The Romance of Missionary Heroism*.

yourself in good—if unusual—company. The unity of faith and purpose among God's people stands out all the more for the diversity of our backgrounds and circumstances.

FROM SORCERERS TO SAINTS

A female Hawaiian chief and a British minister may seem to have little in common, but in the 19th century they faced down the same forces by the power of the same God. The work that 'Opukaha'ia, a Hawaiian runaway, began when he first told his story on the steps of Yale College reached its fulfillment when Chief Kapi'olani challenged the goddess Pele and her sorcerers to a duel of power in a volcano crater. William Brett encountered natural dangers in Guyana like alligators, anacondas, mosquito-borne diseases and even an alligator fighting an anaconda in a mosquito-infested jungle. He also faced danger from sorcerers, who had already lethally poisoned one missionary family. Since the days of the apostle Paul, Christians who have taken the gospel to new places (including Europe and the British Isles) have faced similar challenges. Some of your own ancestors may have been just as hostile to the gospel and its messengers as the local people described in these stories. Perhaps they were similarly transformed.

FROM SORCERERS TO SAINTS

CHAPTER ONE

FROM THE STEPS OF YALE TO THE SLOPES OF KILAUEA

'OPUKAHA'IA AND KAPI'OLANI IN HAWAII

'OPUKAHA'IA'S TEARS

ONE MORNING IN THE second decade of the 19th century, as some Yale students passed up the college steps on their way to their classrooms, they found sitting at the entrance door a dark-skinned lad who was crying silently. When they asked who he was and what was wrong, he told them in broken English a story at once strange and sad.

His name was 'Opukaha'ia, and he was a native of the Hawaiian Islands. In one of the constant intertribal fights, his home had been destroyed by the victors and his father and mother killed before his eyes. Taking his infant brother on his back, he had tried to escape, but was soon noticed, pursued and overtaken. A spear was ruthlessly thrust through the body of the child he carried, while he himself was seized and dragged away into slavery.

'Opukaha'ia gained his liberty by hiding on board an American ship which had called at Hawaii and was homeward bound for New Haven, Connecticut. On the long voyage around Cape Horn, he was treated kindly enough, but when the vessel reached its destination, he was of no use to anyone and was turned adrift to follow his own devices. As he roamed about the town wondering what was to become of him, he came to Yale College and saw the bands of students passing in and out. In the few words of English which he had picked up from the sailors, he asked a passerby what that great building was and why those young men kept coming and going. He was told that this was a school of learning and that those who entered its walls did so that wise men might teach them all that it was best to know.

In this youth from Hawaii, with his restless eyes and broken English, there burned an eager longing to learn. It seemed natural to him to turn his feet toward the college, since there, it seemed, the fountain of truth and knowledge was to be found. But when he climbed the steps and reached the portal, his heart failed him utterly. That was why the students found him crouching at the entrance that morning with tears rolling down his cheeks. There were kind men among his questioners and many kind and Christian hearts among the good folk of the old Puritan town. An interest was awakened in 'Opukaha'ia, which led to his being provided for and taught not only the basics of an American education, but also the great saving truths of the Christian faith.

'OPUKAHA'IA'S MISSION

After some years had passed, 'Opukaha'ia felt that he must go back to his own islands and tell his people the good news that he had learned himself. Meanwhile, the story of this Hawaiian youth had become widely known, and an interest in him and his country had grown up among the American churches. The American Board of Foreign Missions took up the matter and decided to begin missionary work in the Hawaiian Islands. The plan was entered into with a great deal of popular enthusiasm. And when, at length, in 1820, the pioneers set sail on their long voyage round the South American continent, the party included no fewer than 17 persons besides 'Opukaha'ia himself.

In a very real sense, 'Opukaha'ia may be looked upon as the founder of the American mission in Hawaii. If he had not sat weeping some years before on the doorstep of Yale College, that band of missionaries would never have sailed for those far-off islands. But here his share in the enterprise comes to an end. He was not destined to carry the gospel to his countrymen. 'Opukaha'ia died of a decline. It was thought at the time that the harsh

New England winters had been too much for one born amidst the soft, warm breezes of the Pacific Ocean. And so it was left to others to carry out the idea, which his mind had been the first to conceive, of giving to the Hawaiian people the blessings of Christianity.

Perhaps there has never been in the whole history of Protestant missions another record of such rapid and wholesale transformation of an entire people group as took place in connection with this enterprise which had been inspired by the strange vision of a Hawaiian Islander knocking at the gates of a Christian college.[3] The Rev. Titus Coan, for example, one of the leading figures of that stirring period, baptized more than 1,700 persons on a single Sunday and in one year received considerably more than 5,000 men and women into the full communion of the Church. People who up to the time of their conversion had lived a lawless life—robbers, murderers, drunkards, the former high priests of a cruel idolatry, "their hands but recently washed from the blood of human victims"—all assembled together in Christian peace and love to partake of the sacrament of the Lord's Supper. And yet, sudden as it was, this was no transient emotional result. It was a reconstruction of the community from its very base.

KAPI'OLANI'S TRANSFORMATION

Of all the arresting incidents of this great religious revolution, the most dramatic is one which took place within the very crater of Kilauea, the largest and most awful of the active volcanoes of the world.[4] In this dread amphitheater, on the very brink of the eternal "Fire Fountains of Hawaii," Kapi'olani, the high chieftainess of Ka'awaloa, openly challenged and defied Pele, the indwelling goddess of the volcano, as every Hawaiian believed.

In 1825, one of the missionaries, the Rev. Mr. Bishop, made a preaching tour right round the main island of Hawaii. An

3. Yale College (originally called the Collegiate School) was founded in 1701 by a group of ministers so that students would be prepared for "Publick employment both in Church and Civil State."
4. Mauna Loa, located just 20 miles from Kilauea on the Island of Hawaii, is now considered the largest active volcano in the world.

adventurous tour it was, for he constantly had to clamber on hands and knees up the face of precipitous cliffs and to make his way over rugged lava beds or across deep gullies and swollen mountain torrents. At other times it was necessary to skirt the frowning rocky coast in a frail canoe so as to circumvent those inland barriers which could not be crossed. The villages were often difficult to find, hidden as they were in almost inaccessible glens. But whenever this brave, adventurous preacher stood face to face with the people, the most wonderful results followed and he was amply repaid for all his dangers and toils.

Among the converts of that time was Kapi'olani, the most noted of all the female chiefs of Hawaii. She ruled over large possessions in the southern part of the main island. Previous to this, she had been intensely superstitious and had lived a reckless and intemperate life. Now she was utterly changed. First, she set herself to reform her own life, dismissing all her husbands but one, who like herself professed Christianity, and adopting strictly sober habits. Next, she did her utmost to uproot idolatrous notions and customs among her people, putting down infanticide, murder, drunkenness and robbery with a firm hand and without counting the possible cost to herself.

KAPI'OLANI'S MISSION

Kapi'olani soon realized that the great obstacle to the progress of the gospel among the Hawaiians was their faith in the divinities of Kilauea, and above all in Pele herself. That grim and terrible goddess was supposed to have her dwelling place within the crater of the burning mountain. Pele had a retinue of priests and prophets, both male and female, whose hold upon the popular imagination was nothing short of tremendous.

Their false teaching seemed to be reinforced by the great volcano with its smoking summit, an ever-present reality in the eyes of all. Its frequent eruptions revealed the might of the unseen goddess. The deep thunders of Kilauea were Pele's own voice. The long filaments spun by the wind from the liquid lava and tossed over the edge of the crater were Pele's dusky, streaming hair. And those priests and priestesses who offered daily sacrifice to her divinity were the living oracles of her will. Kapi'olani saw quite clearly that the power of the fire goddess must be broken before Christianity could spread in Hawaii. She accordingly resolved to challenge that power in its innermost stronghold and sanctuary by defying Pele to her face on the very floor of the crater of Kilauea.

When Kapiʻolani announced her intention to her followers, they did everything they could to hold her back from such a project. Even her husband, though himself a professed Christian, begged her to abstain from a deed so rash and dangerous. But to all expostulations she had one reply. "All taboos," she said, "are done away. We are safe in the keeping of the Almighty God, and no power of earth or hell can harm His servants." When her people saw how determined she was they gave up trying to dissuade her. About 80 of them were even so bold as to volunteer to accompany her to the summit of the fiery mountain.

From Kapiʻolani's home, Kilauea was distant about 100 miles in a straight line. To reach it was a toilsome journey which took her and her companions over jagged mountain peaks and rough lava beds. But no detour would she make. She pressed straight on toward the volcano, over which there ever hung a dark pall of smoke by day and a lurid cloud of fire by night. As she advanced, people came in crowds out of the valleys to watch the progress of this strange pilgrimage. Many of them implored her to turn back before it was too late and not to draw down upon herself and others the vengeance of the fire gods. But this was her invariable reply: "If I am destroyed, you may all believe in Pele; but if I am not destroyed, you must all turn to the only true God."

At length, after a most fatiguing march, this bold champion of the new faith reached the base of Kilauea and began the upward ascent. As Kapiʻolani approached the cone, one of Pele's prophetesses appeared and warned her back in the name of the goddess. In her hand the prophetess held a piece of white bark-cloth, and as she waved it above her head, she declared it to be a message from Pele herself. "Read the message!" exclaimed Kapiʻolani, upon which the woman held the pretended oracle before her and poured out a flood of gibberish, which she declared to be an ancient sacred dialect.

Kapiʻolani smiled. "You have delivered a message from your god," she said, "which none of us can understand. I will read you a message from my God which everyone will understand."

Whereupon she opened her Hawaiian Bible and read several passages that told of Jehovah's almighty power and of the heavenly Father's saving love in Jesus Christ.

Defying the Goddess of the Volcano

Still pressing on, Kapi'olani came at length to the very edge of the vast crater, which lies 1,000 feet below the summit of the enclosing cone, and led the way down the precipitous descent toward the black lava bed. On the crater's brink there grew clusters of the refreshing *ohelo* berry, sacred to Pele herself, which no Hawaiian of those days would taste till he had first cast a laden branch down the precipice toward the fiery lake, saying as he did so, "Pele, here are your *ohelos*. I offer some to you; some I also eat." This formula was supposed to render the eating safe and without it an awful taboo would be infringed.

Seeing the berries hanging all around her, Kapi'olani stopped and ate of them freely without making any acknowledgment to the goddess. She then made her way slowly down into the bowl of the crater of Halema'uma'u, the "House of Everlasting Burning." When she reached the bottom, she walked across the hardened crust of lava till she came to the center. Standing there, she picked up broken fragments of lava and flung them defiantly toward the seething cauldron, which writhed and moaned and flung out long hissing tongues of red and purple flame.

Having thus desecrated Pele's holy of holies in the most dreadful manner of which a Hawaiian imagination could conceive, Kapi'olani now turned to her trembling followers, who stood at some distance behind. In a loud clear voice, she spoke these words, which were engraved forever afterwards on the memories of all who heard them: "My God is Jehovah. He it was who kindled these fires. I do not fear Pele. Should I perish by her wrath, then you may fear her power. But if Jehovah saves me while I am breaking her taboos, then you must fear and love Him. The gods of Hawaii are vain."

Kapi'olani then called upon her people to kneel down and offer a solemn act of adoration to the One Almighty God and thereafter to join their voices with hers in a hymn of joyful praise. And so, by Christian praise and prayer the very crater of Kilauea, formerly the supposed abode of a cruel goddess, was consecrated as a temple to the God of holiness and love.

THE GOSPEL'S IMPACT

The news of Kapi'olani's bold deed soon ran from end to end in Hawaii. It sent a shiver of despair though the hearts of Pele's priests and devoted followers. Everyone felt that the old dominion of the fire gods must be tottering to its fall. Before long, the people began to turn in crowds from their idolatries. In the larger centers of population, Hawaiians gathered in vast multitudes to listen to the missionaries. More than once Mr. Bishop preached to assemblages that numbered upwards of 10,000 people. Other chiefs and chieftainesses followed Kapi'olani's example by openly professing their Christian faith. Even the heathen priests and priestesses renounced their allegiance to dark and bloody altars and made profession of their faith in Christ.

One day, a sinister figure presented itself before one of the missionaries among a number of people who were waiting to receive Christian instruction. It was a man whose gruesome office it had been, in the service of Pele's altar, to hunt and catch the victims that were needed for the human sacrifices demanded by the goddess. This dreadful being had acquired the skill of a wild beast in lurking in the bypaths of the forests to leap upon the passersby. He was possessed of such enormous strength that he could break the bones of his victims by simply enfolding them in his iron embrace. No wonder that on seeing him the people shrank back in terror as if from some monster of the jungle. But even this man was conquered by the gospel of love and peace and turned from serving Pele to follow Jesus Christ.

The sudden glory of a Christian dawn rose upon the Hawaiian Islands, flushing mountain, shore and ocean with the radiance of the skies. So long as men tell the wonderful story of the spread of Christianity over the islands of Oceania and recall the heroes and heroines of the past, the figure of Kapi'olani will stand out bravely as she is seen in the strength of her newborn faith, defying Pele's wrath in the dark crater of Kilauea.

•••

Source Material. The story of the American Mission to Hawaii, and in particular the incident of Kapi'olani's challenge to the fire goddess, was drawn almost entirely from Miss C. F. Gordon Cumming's *Fire Fountains: The Kingdom of Hawaii* (William Blackwood and Sons, 1883), which she generously permitted John C. Lambert to make free use of for the purposes of his book.

CHAPTER 2

BEAUTIFUL FEET COME TO BEAUTIFUL HAIR

WILLIAM BRETT IN GUYANA

A LAND OF MANY WATERS

IN THE FORESTS OF BRITISH GUIANA[5] the Society for the Propagation of the Gospel long carried on a most interesting work among the Caribs, Arawaks, Waraoons and other tribes around whom gathers so much of the adventure and tragedy of early West Indian history. None of the Society's agents was more diligent or successful than the Rev. William Henry Brett. We shall follow Mr. Brett as he tells us something of his canoe voyages on the rivers of the Essequibo district, of his journeys on foot through the tropical forests and swamps, of dangers from pumas and jaguars by land and alligators and snakes by water, of the ways and thoughts of the local tribes and the power of religious truth to deliver them from the tyranny of immemorial superstitions.

Ministry among the native peoples of Guiana was beset in the early days by many serious difficulties. One was the wild character of the people and their hostility, the hostility especially of their sorcerers, to the teachers of a new religion. Not the least of the difficulties was that of traveling in such a country. It involved laborious and often dangerous journeys by foot and canoe

---

5. Present-day Guyana, South America.

through dense forests which at certain seasons were converted into dismal swamps. But Mr. Brett had the true enthusiasm and pluck of the pioneer missionary and seems to have considered the hardships that fell to his lot as all "in the day's work."

Guiana is a land of many rivers, and this makes canoeing the chief method of traveling, especially as the forests themselves become inundated after the rains. It is then possible to cross from river to river by means of passages called *itabbos*. It is not all plain sailing, however, in a voyage of this kind. Every few minutes, travelers have to use their cutlasses to lop away the network of interlacing branches and creepers which the abundant growth of the tropics weaves so quickly from side to side on the narrow waterway.

Canoeing was not always feasible, and then would begin the tramp through the forests. To the inexperienced traveler in this wilderness of rank vegetation majestically confused, there sometimes came the fear of being lost, for he felt his own helplessness as to direction and knew that, but for the instinct of his local guides, he would soon go utterly astray. He was often bewildered, too, by the multiplicity of strange sounds. Parrots screeched, monkeys chattered, cicadas piped on a high note which suggested a shrill steam whistle, insects innumerable chirped and whirred. At times there came a noise like a muffled crash of thunder which told that some ancient giant of the woods had fallen at last.

The forests of Guiana are full of swamps, and when Mr. Brett came to these, there was nothing for it but to take off his shoes and socks, sling them round his neck and wade on through mud and slime. Repeated soakings often made his feet swell so badly that it was hardly possible to pinch them into shoes again and he found it easier simply to go barefooted like the local people. But this also had its disadvantages, for alternate wading through marshes and walking with bare feet over the burning sandy soil brought on painful sores which, unless great care was taken, would pass into ulcers.

Sometimes the swamps were so deep that they could not be waded and the only means of crossing was by trees cut down and thrown across. These primitive forest bridges, which were also used for crossing the smaller streams and ravines, were often of considerable length. Mr. Brett tells of one which he measured, the trunk of a *mora* tree, which was 108 feet long from the place where the trunk was cut to the point at which the lowest branches began to spring. The locals were quite expert at walking on these slippery pathways, but to a European with his boots on they presented a formidable task.

A LAND OF MANY CREATURES

Apart from the malarial fevers to which in those low-lying tropical regions a European is constantly liable, the chief dangers encountered by Mr. Brett in his journeys into the interior came from the wild animals which swarmed in Guiana, both on land and water. There were alligators of various sorts which, as amphibious creatures, are dangerous on both elements. Mr. Brett told of one which made its nest in his own churchyard and rushed savagely one evening at an assembly of mourners gathered round a grave just after he had finished reading the burial service, scattering them in all directions.

A Titanic Combat

But not less dreaded than the alligator was the great anaconda, or *camudi*, a species of water boa which swims like an eel and grows to the length of 30 feet. In the water, the *camudi* is more than a match for the alligator and has been known to even attack people inside a canoe. One Sunday morning, an exciting fight took place midstream between a *camudi* and an alligator, exactly in front of a chapel on the bank of the river Pomeroon in which Mr. Brett was conducting a service. At the news of the fight his congregation deserted him, and even he could not resist the temptation to follow them as speedily as possible to the scene of action.

The battle went on desperately for a long time, but at last the *camudi* succeeded in getting that deadly grip with its tail which gives it full purchase for its gigantic strength, and then it drew its coils tighter and tighter round the body of its formidable antagonist until the life of the alligator seemed to be completely squeezed out. At this point one of the onlookers, who had a gun and was a good marksman, fired and killed the *camudi*. It sank to the bottom. The alligator drifted ashore by and by with its ribs crushed in, nearly dead, and it too was quickly dispatched.

Dangers lurked on land as well as in the water. Besides the *labaria*, a very deadly snake which lurks among bushes or in the holes of old trees, the traveler through the forests had always to be on his guard against the puma and the jaguar. But there were smaller creatures of the tropics for which humans and the rifle held no terror. There were myriad butterflies, of course, which fluttered past on wings of crimson and gold; darting hummingbirds, with ruby or emerald breasts gleaming in the sunlight; fireflies which came out at dusk and flitted to and fro with their soft twinkling lights in the warm night air that was heavy with the breath of flowers. If the tiny creatures of the tropic woods were all like these, the traveler might have fancied himself in a kind of earthly paradise.

But what of the *marabuntas*, which Trinidad boys used to call "marrowbones," from the idea that the stings of these fierce wasps could penetrate that far? What of scorpions, centipedes, tarantulas, bloodsucking bats, jiggers and biting ants, whether black, white or red? Worst of all, what of the ubiquitous, irrepressible, unconquerable mosquito, which sometimes almost drives its victims mad and whose victories over man, its mortal foe, deserve to be sung in the notes of its own musical humming and written with the blood of its helpless victims in some epic of the jungle? Mr. Brett did not exaggerate in the least when he reckoned insects and other small annoyances among the most serious trials of missionary life in the inland districts of British Guiana.

A LAND OF MANY PEOPLES

Another difficulty for Mr. Brett and other missionaries was caused by language. Travelers, as they left the coast and plunged into the forest, passed rapidly from one tribe to another, all speaking different tongues. Nearest to the sea were the Waraoons and the Arawaks. Farther inland were the Caribs. Beyond these were the migratory Acawoios, who did not live in villages but wandered through the woods. With their deadly blowpipes they brought down from the highest trees the birds, monkeys and other animals that they used for food. Mr. Brett, who ministered for decades in Guiana, found it necessary to learn four local languages, none of which had ever before been reduced to a written form. And not only did he master them for himself, but he prepared grammars and vocabularies which made the task of his successors infinitely easier and also translated into all of them large parts of the New Testament.

Among all the tribes of Guiana, *piai* men, or sorcerers, were the priests of religion. No one dared to oppose them in anything, for they were experts in poisons and their enemies had a way of dying suddenly. In sickness, the most implicit confidence was placed in a *piai* man's powers, which to some extent were medicinal no doubt (for he generally had a real acquaintance with the healing virtues of the plants of the forest) but to a much greater degree were supposed to be supernatural. His special function was to drive away the evil spirit that had taken possession of the sick man. This he did by rattling a hollow calabash gourd containing some fragments of rock crystal (an instrument of magical efficacy and the peculiar symbol of the *piai* man's office), by chanting a round of monotonous incantations and by fumigating the patient plentifully with tobacco smoke, which was believed to exert a potent, if mysterious, influence.

THE GOD OF EVERY PEOPLE

It was naturally from these *piai* men that the strongest resistance came to the introduction of Christianity among the tribes of Guiana. Not long before Mr. Brett arrived, a missionary family received a deadly gift of poisoned food from one of those sorcerers. Mr. Brett was frequently warned that the sorcerers were going to *piai* him also. Instead, a strange thing happened.

Saccibarra, whose name means "Beautiful Hair," was the chief of the Arawaks and their leading sorcerer. He became disgusted with the tricks and hypocrisies of his profession and broke his *marakka*, or magical calabash rattle. He came to Mr. Brett's hut asking to be taught about "the Great Our Father, who dwelleth in heaven." After a time, he was baptized, and it was with his aid that Mr. Brett was able to carry through his first efforts at Scripture translation.

Making Poisoned Arrows in British Guiana

Still better things ensued, for five other sorcerers followed Saccibarra's example, gave up their *marakkas* to Mr. Brett in token that they had renounced the practice of magic and became faithful members of the Christian Church. Evangelists arose among the local people. Soon chapels sprang up here and there in the depths of the forest—two of them, as was accidentally discovered at a later stage, having been built on ancient cannibal mounds. Struck by the appearance of these mounds, Mr. Brett was led to undertake a little excavation. His research speedily proved that the very spots where Christ's gospel was preached had once been the kitchen trash heaps for large cannibal villages. There, piled together, were the skulls and other bones of human beings slaughtered long ago, these skulls and bones being invariably cracked and split in a way which showed that the hungry cannibals in their horrible feasts had eaten the very brains and marrow of their victims.

In the Pomeroon district of Guiana, the center of Mr. Brett's labors, more than 5,000 persons were brought into the Church through baptism. As for the moral and spiritual effect of his patient exertions, we may cite the testimony of the Pomeroon civil magistrate, who at first did not encourage Christian work among the local tribes:

"A more disorderly people than the Arawaks," he wrote, "could not be found in any part of Guiana. Murders and violent cases of assault were of frequent occurrence. Now the case is reversed. They attend regularly divine service, their children are educated, they themselves dress neatly, are lawfully married, and as a body there are no people in point of general good conduct to surpass them. This change, which has caused peace and contentment to prevail, was brought about solely by missionary labor."

Even from the most external point of view, missions is full of heroism and adventure. But to those who look deeper, the spiritual drama is the most wonderful—the transformation of character and life, the turning of a sinner into a Christian.

•••

Source Material. The chief authority for this chapter was Mr. Brett's *Mission Work Among the Indian Tribes in the Forests of Guiana* (London: Society for Promoting Christian Knowledge, ca. 1880). Reference was also made, however, for some points to *Ten Years of Mission Life in British Guiana* by the Rev. W. T. Veness (London: Society for Promoting Christian Knowledge, 1869) and *Protestant Missions in South America*, by Canon F. P. L. Josa and others (New York: Student Volunteer Movement, 1900).

PART II

CALL AND RESPONSE

Fred Arnot and James Evans both received direct invitations to their places of ministry, but not from the people or for the reasons that you might expect. Mr. Arnot was already an experienced traveler on the African continent when he met messengers of King Msidi in search of white men to live in his kingdom. Msidi meant European traders, but Arnot decided to respond anyway. Mr. Evans was teaching school on Lake Ontario when a request for missionaries came from the directors of the Hudson Trading Company, of all people. Both invitations were economically motivated, but that didn't stop God from using them. Today, God still uses economics, politics and many other circumstances to strategically deploy His messengers from the Arctic to the African desert and everywhere in between.

CHAPTER 3

WHEN BIRCH BARK TALKED

JAMES EVANS IN CANADA

A CALL TO THE WILD

WE HAVE NOW TO FOLLOW the story of the Reverend James Evans and his journeys and adventures amid the "snowflakes and sunbeams" of the far north, from Lake Superior to the Arctic Circle. He pushed ever forward as a pioneer of Christianity to the native peoples of British North America. Modernization has done little more than fringe the borders of those vast territories of the Canadian Northwest through which he journeyed unweariedly, whether in the long winter or the short summer, bearing his message of peace and goodwill.

James Evans was an Englishman who had gone to Canada in search of a career. Finding it difficult to get employment in business, he became a backwoods schoolmaster. It was a fine training for the life that lay before him, bringing not only experience as a teacher, but familiarity with those arts of the hardy backwoodsman which were, by and by, to stand him in good stead.

Mr. Evans was a Wesleyan, and as the leaders of the Wesleyan Church in Canada came to know his talents and enterprise, as well as his Christian zeal, they offered him a post as teacher in one of their schools for indigenous children in the Lake Ontario district. It was pioneer work of the purest kind, but Evans thoroughly enjoyed it. His success as a missionary teacher led, before long, to his being ordained as a minister and appointed to labor

31

among the tribes on the northern shores of Lake Superior.

To any ordinary man, the far-stretching coasts of the largest of all the Great Lakes would have been a field sufficient for a life's labors. But Evans was not an ordinary man. He was never satisfied unless he was continually pressing on into new regions and carrying the name of Jesus Christ where it had not been heard before. And in the most unexpected way, there came an opening and a call to a new and larger sphere such as he longed for.

The Land of "Snowflakes and Sunbeams"

The fur traders of the Hudson Bay Company, whose forts were scattered right across the continent from the Atlantic to the Pacific, and from the Great Lakes to the Arctic Ocean, had noticed for some time that many of the indigenous tribes of the north were drifting steadily southwards. This gave them much concern, for it was from the northern part of their territories that they got a large proportion of their most valuable furs. This southerly movement of the hunters threatened the Company with serious loss.

At first, the migration was set down simply to a desire to escape to a more genial climate, but fuller investigation revealed that the true reason was very different. The peoples of the north had heard of a new and wonderful religion which had come to their brothers in the south—a religion given by the Great Spirit to the red man as well as to the white. Around many a campfire the tidings had been discussed. At last, religious curiosity became so strong that, in the words of Mr. Egerton Young (the biographer of Mr. Evans), "family after family embarked in their birch canoes and started for the land of the South Wind, in order to find the teacher and the Book."

It occurred to the directors of the Hudson Bay Company that it would be to their advantage to bring missionaries to the tribes instead of leaving them to go in search of a missionary. They applied accordingly to the Wesleyans in England to send without delay several suitable men to work among the peoples of the Northwest. This the Wesleyan Society at once proceeded to do. As the most competent man to be the leader of the movement, their choice fell upon Mr. Evans.

THE PRAYING-MASTER

On reaching his destination, Evans was soon plunged into the kind of work he delighted in, for here were native peoples from far and near. Those of the district around the fort were called Swampy Crees. They believed in a Kissa-Manetoo or Good God, but also and still more strongly in a Muche-Manetoo or Evil Spirit, whose power was thought to be the greater of the two. They listened eagerly to the good news which the white preacher brought to their wigwams of a divine love which conquers all evil, and a Father in heaven to whom every one of His children, whatever color their skin, is equally dear. It was more difficult, however, for the Ayumeaoolcemoii, or "praying-master," as Evans was called, to convince them to give up their hatreds and cruelties and other wicked ways.

A chief named Maskepetoon, a man of magnificent stature and strength, liked Mr. Evans greatly but said that this new religion was only fit for old women. "I will never be a Christian," he cried, "so long as there is a scalp to take or a horse to steal from the Blackfeet." Maskepetoon was a man of such an ungovernable temper that he scalped one of his own wives in a fit of displeasure. And yet this same chief, by and by, met the murderer of his son on the prairie. Riding up to him, tomahawk in hand, Maskepetoon said, "By all the laws of the tribes you deserve to die. But I have learned that if we expect the Great Spirit to forgive us, we must forgive our enemies, and therefore I forgive you."

Eventually, Mr. Evans began to turn his attention to those

far-off tribes which had their settlements along the foothills of the Rocky Mountains or the banks of the Mackenzie River. Now began his great expeditions by waterway or dog trail. Evans would undertake a circuit of 5,000 or 6,000 miles in a single season. He toiled upstream in his canoe and darted down swift rapids with a thrill of dangerous delight. He camped out on the rolling plains of the far west, which were then the special preserves of the buffalo. Sometimes, as he lay down at night, the roaring of the bulls in the immediate neighborhood was so loud and incessant that it was impossible to fall asleep. And often, as he closed his eyes, he knew that if the herd should be seized with a sudden panic and stampede in the direction of his little camp, nothing could save him and his companions from being trampled to death.

Maskepetoon Forgives

It is Evans's winter journeys by dog train over the frozen snow that strike us most with a sense of adventure and daring. His favorite team of dogs was famous all over the land. They were hybrids—half dogs, half wolves—possessed of such strength that they could travel 80 or 90 miles a day dragging a load of 300 pounds or more. In harness they were easily controlled, and yet they were so fierce that they had always to be chained up at night. Through the summer they were carefully shut up in a high stockade. Their savage disposition eventually brought about their death. One morning, an old chief who had come to look for Mr. Evans opened the gate of the stockade yard, thinking he might be inside. In a moment, the dogs sprang upon him and mangled him to death before they could be beaten off. For this crime they were immediately shot.

ALL IN A DAY'S TRAVEL

Let us take one or two glimpses of a tour in the depths of winter. The sledge which glided so swiftly over the snow was shaped like a boy's toboggan, eight or 10 feet long and about 18 inches broad, and was drawn by a team of four powerful dogs. On a long journey, two or three sledges were necessary, for a plentiful supply of provisions had to be carried, as well as bedding and camping utensils. As the train swept forward, there was often not a landmark to be seen— nothing from horizon to horizon but a vast unbroken sheet of snow.

Traveling was trying enough when the air was at 40, 50 or even 60 degrees below zero, though infinitely worse when accompanied by a wind sufficiently strong to raise the fine, powdery snow into a blinding, choking blizzard. After a long day's drive, both men and dogs were thankful to stop and enjoy rest, warmth and food. The camp was nothing more than a square hole in the deep snow, scooped out with snowshoes that served as shovels. On three sides the snow was banked up, while on the fourth a huge fire was kindled with logs cut from the forest.

Kettles were filled with snow, and as soon as the snow melted over the fire, a goodly hunk of frozen buffalo or bear or beaver was popped in to be boiled. Meat taken out of the boiling kettle froze so fast that it had sometimes to be thrust back into the water two or three times in the course of a meal. The tea was flavored with milk which was presented, not in a milk jug, but in a bag, from which pieces of it were broken off with a hatchet as required. If the tea was not quickly drunk it could not be drunk at all, having already become solid. Meanwhile, the dogs were fed, mostly with frozen fish which had first to be thawed before the fire. If the night was unusually cold, they were allowed to get on their dog shoes, which were not unlike socks. For the privilege of getting on their shoes they often begged by howling.

Winter Camp

After evening prayers came the process of going, or rather being put, to bed. The local people had a knack of rolling themselves up securely in a warm rug of rabbit skins, but a foreigner was the better for being tucked in. Mr. Evans's travel companions spread blankets and rugs over him and tucked in his head as well as his shoulders and feet, leaving not the least chink for the entrance of the outer air at any point. Under such treatment Mr. Evans felt at first as if he were being suffocated, but he soon learned to adjust himself to the necessary conditions of safety. There was a real danger to the sleeper in neglecting these precautions. Mr. Young, the biographer, tells of one restless traveler who could not lie still in his camp bed and so shook his face free from the protecting blankets. Wakening by and by, he put his hand up and felt what he took to be the icy handle of an axe. It turned out to be his own frozen nose.

On a long march, Mr. Evans frequently slept during the day and traveled through the night. The reason for this was that the intense white glare of the snow, with the sunshine reflected from it, was apt to bring on a distressing complaint of the eyes called snow blindness. Besides, to a lover of nature, there was a peculiar charm about the winter nights, especially in the sub-Arctic zone. Those northern nights were nearly always beautiful, whether the moon was flooding the world with a soft radiance, or the frosty stars sparkled like diamonds through an atmosphere of absolute purity, or the aurora flashed and blazed, filling even those who had seen it times without number with a sense of awe in the presence of a glory so unearthly.

WHEN BIRCH BARK TALKED

But from the wanderings of the "Apostle of the North" we must pass to notice another feature of his varied activities. He was not only an intrepid and indefatigable traveler, but a remarkable linguist and a man also of real inventive genius. A matter which troubled him greatly was the difficulty of teaching the local people to read in the ordinary way. He brooded for years over the problem of inventing a simpler and easier path than that of the alphabet and the spelling book, and at last hit upon the plan which is known as the Cree Syllabic System. Taking the Cree language as his model, he found that it contained only 36 principal sounds. By devising simple characters to represent these sounds, he made it possible for any Cree who learned to identify the characters to read at once without further difficulty.

The result was that in a very few days, old and young alike were able to read. But next came the difficulty of supplying them with books. Evans had no materials for printing and no experience in work of this kind. He begged from the traders at the fort the thin sheets of lead with which their tea chests were lined. Then, having carved out models of his syllabic characters and made casts of them in clay, he melted the lead and poured it into the molds. And so, after many failures, he obtained a sufficient supply of type. Ink he manufactured out of soot mixed with sturgeon oil. Paper he could neither get nor make, but he found that sheets of birch bark would serve his purpose very well. Finally, in lieu of a printing press, he begged the loan of a jack screw used for packing bales of furs and turned out the first books which his flock had ever seen.

37

The excitement produced by these printed sheets of bark was immense, for it seemed to the people nothing less than magic that birch bark could "talk," and something still more wonderful that it could bring them a message from the Great Spirit Himself. The result was that thousands, young and old, became readers of God's Word. When the Society in England realized the value of Mr. Evans's invention, he was furnished with a properly equipped printing press, from which, year by year, there came a steady supply of Bibles and Testaments in the native tongue.

"The syllabic characters," wrote Mr. Young years later, "are still in use. The British and Foreign Bible Society now furnish all these Northern missions with Bibles and Testaments free of cost. Hundreds of Indians are reading out of them every day of the year. Missionaries to other tribes have utilized these syllabics for other languages by adding additional signs for sounds not found among the Crees. Methodists, Episcopalians, Moravians, Roman Catholics and others use these syllabics of James Evans, and find them of incalculable value."

INSTINCTS OF LOVE AND OF GRIEF

As illustrating both the remarkable character of the hero of this chapter and the kind of influence he exerted, a tragic incident in his history is worthy of notice. One day, Mr. Evans was out in a canoe shooting ducks along with a young Chippewayan[6] man named Hassel, who had become a Christian. By some accident which he never understood, Evans's gun went off. The full charge entered the head of poor Hassel, who fell back dead into the canoe.

Mr. Evans's grief was terrible and was compounded by the fact that the Chippewayan were largely unbelieving and retained their traditional beliefs and customs. They held that blood must be given for blood and life for life. Evans's sorrow and sense of responsibility for his companion's death made him feel that he must surrender himself to Hassel's relatives, even though it might result in his being put to death himself. Accordingly, he wound up all his personal affairs, and after a trying scene of farewell with his wife and daughter,

---

6. Now usually referred to as Ojibwe.

set out all alone for the distant part of the country in which the Chippeways lived.

Reaching the encampment of the tribe, he asked for the wigwam of Hassel's father. When it was pointed out to him, he entered, and sitting down on the ground told his sad story, tears of sorrow meanwhile trickling down his face. At once, the tent was full of excitement. Grasping their tomahawks and drawing their knives, the men of the family cried out for the blood of this foreigner who had slain their kinsman.

But there was one person in the tent who had already resolved that the foreigner should live. This was no other than Hassel's mother. She had been stricken with anguish when she heard of her son's death, but she had watched the stranger's countenance and listened to his voice as he told his story. She knew by the instincts of love and of grief that Evans was the true friend of her boy, and that his sorrow for what had happened was not less sincere than her own. When the avengers of blood were about to spring upon him, she ran forward and, putting both her hands on his head, said firmly, "He shall not die. There was no evil in his heart. He loved my son. He shall live, and shall be my son in the place of the one who is not among the living."

And so, the Christian missionary was actually adopted, after the local custom, into the tribe and family of the Chippeways. For a time, he remained in the wigwam with his new father and mother. After he returned to his own family and work, he still regarded himself as their son, given them in place of the son he had shot. Mr. Evans knew that Hassel, after becoming a Christian, had been very thoughtful of his parents and had sent them a present from time to time. And though himself a poor man, Evans made a point to the end of his life of sending regularly to his foster parents what he regarded as their rightful share of his own yearly income.

•••

Source Material. *The Apostle of the North: Rev. James Evans*, by Egerton R. Young (London: Marshall Brothers, 1899) and *Hudson Bay*, by R. M. Ballantyne (London: Thomas Nelson and Sons, [1848?]).

CHAPTER 4

WATER FROM SAND

FRED ARNOT IN THE CONGO

INVITATION TO A TRAVELER

IN THE EARLY 1880S a young Scotchman, Fred S. Arnot by name, was traveling from the Upper Zambesi[7] toward the West African coast. He met a company of men from the far interior with a letter in their charge. The letter was sent by Msidi, king of Garenganze,[8] and contained an earnest appeal that white men would come to his country. Arnot did not doubt that by "white men" King Msidi meant European traders, by whom he and his people might be enriched. Arnot was no trader, but a pioneer missionary who had already crossed Africa from east to west seeking to do good to the local peoples. At that very time, he was wondering where it would be best for him to settle down more permanently as a Christian teacher.

Mr. Arnot may be described as one of the most remarkable of the many heroes of African travel, not so much for what he actually accomplished as for the manner and spirit in which he accomplished it. His methods of progress were not those of the well-equipped and hustling explorer, but of the lonely wanderer who makes his way quietly, patiently and in the spirit of love,

---

7. The Zambesi is the fourth-longest river in Africa. The upper portion is located near where present-day Zambia, Angola and the Democratic Republic of the Congo meet.
8. The area around the southern part of present-day DRC.

from village to village and from tribe to tribe. He had already served his apprenticeship to African travel. Landing in Natal[9] in 1881, he had slowly trekked through the Orange Free State and the Transvaal to Khama's country, had next crossed the awful Kalahari Desert and so made his way to the Zambesi.

A whole year was occupied in this journey, which brought with it many experiences of danger and suffering. Repeatedly he had been on the point of perishing from hunger or thirst. Once, after marching in the desert for three days and nights without a drop of water, he met some Bushmen[10] who supplied him with a drink after their own fashion. They dug a pit in the sand and sank long tubes made of reeds into the ground at the bottom. By and by, water began to gather, as they knew it would, at the sunk end of the tube. They invited Arnot to drink. He tried, but was quite unable to suck the water up the long tube. The Bushmen, whom frequent practice had made adept in the art, sucked it up for him and then spat it out into a tortoise shell and handed it to the stranger. "It was frothy stuff," he later wrote, "as you may imagine; but I enjoyed it more than any draught I ever took."

Arnot's ways of getting food had sometimes been peculiar also. On the Zambesi, he often depended for his supper on the crocodiles, which are very plentiful in that great river. Not that he ate those loathsome reptiles, but he was thankful at least to share their meals. When one of the larger game comes down to the river to drink, the crocodile creeps up stealthily, seizes the animal by the nose, drags it under water and then hides the body under the river bank until it becomes almost putrid. When it is "high" enough to suit his taste, Master Croc brings it to the surface and enjoys a feast. A hungry Arnot used to lie on the bank and watch one of those animals as it rose, with perhaps a quarter of an antelope in its jaws. Then he fired at its head and compelled it to drop its supper, and in this way provided himself with his own. He admits that it was anything but a dainty repast.

---

9. Now Durban, South Africa.

10. The indigenous people of South Africa are now often referred to as San, as some consider "Bushman" to be demeaning.

ALL IN A DAY'S JOURNEY

King Msidi's appeal came to Arnot with all the force of a personal call and he made preparations for a march to the Garenganze country, a journey of eight or nine months. Garenganze lies in the very heart of Central Africa, some 1,500 miles each way from the Indian Ocean and the Atlantic. Up to 1886, the year of Arnot's arrival, only two Europeans had visited King Msidi's dominions—a German traveler from the east and a Portuguese from the south. In both cases the visits were very brief.

The earlier stages of Arnot's journey led along a well-trodden route in Portuguese territory. First came a low-lying desert region, which is just at the foot of the hills that mark the beginning of the lower section of the African plateau. After climbing these hills, Arnot found himself for a time in a fertile tropical country. By and by another and a higher tableland rose before him, on climbing which he passed so suddenly out of the climate of the tropics that he could almost mark the line of demarcation between trees like the baobab and the more familiar vegetation of the temperate zone.

Arnot hired local porters and guides along the way. He had no end of difficulty in getting porters to accompany him on his tramp into the unknown regions, which now stretched before him like an unexplored ocean. But at length he succeeded in gathering a sufficient company. Arnot rode on an ox and numbered among his companions a faithful dog and a parrot, which he considered a valuable addition to the resources of an African caravan. Poll, as the parrot was called, was of great service in keeping up the spirits of the travelers. It was a true jokester of a bird, seeming as if it watched for opportunities when there would be some credit in being jolly. When everyone was dull and depressed it would suddenly make some ridiculous remark or break out in imitation of an old man's laugh, relieving the monotony of the march and putting the weary travelers into good humor again.

Once, when the travelers ran low on meat, Arnot seized his gun to hunt game, forgetting that it was already loaded. As he was pulling off the cover, the charge suddenly went off, shattering the point of his left forefinger. There was no one with him who could dress a wound, and he thought it best to get one of the men to cut off the top joint according to his directions.

Arnot recorded for us a clear picture of the daily routine of an African journey. By break of day the camp was astir, for the porters were always anxious to get well along the road in the cool of the morning. Breakfast they did not trouble about, being content to have one good meal at the close of the day. They buckled on their belts, shouldered their loads of 60 pounds each and trotted off through the forest. Often someone began a solo in a high key and all joined lustily in the chorus. One or two halts were made, and there could be considerable delay when rivers had to be crossed. But for the most part, all pressed on steadily for the next camping place, which was generally reached by noon.

When a site for the camp had been fixed upon, some of the party were sent out to the nearest villages to buy food—the staple diet being maize meal made into a thick porridge. Meanwhile, the others busied themselves with erecting shelters for the night. Poles were cut down in the forest and stacked after the manner in which soldiers pile their rifles. Against these, branches were rested, and if it was the rainy season a thatching of the long African grass was added. Then fires were kindled to cook the supper, and these were kept up through the night to scare away wild beasts.

An African camp at night, said Mr. Arnot, would make a fine picture on canvas—the blazing fires; the faces clustered round them; the men singing, talking, laughing and all about a pitchy darkness made doubly deep by the dense shadows of bush and forest. Every night it was Arnot's habit to sit with his men around the campfire, trying to convey to them the purpose of his mission. He felt that it was of the first importance that they should understand his message and his motive in bringing it and so should be able to give an answer to the thousands of local people who would be sure to bombard them with questions as to who this white man was and why he had come.

A Cautious Welcome

Garenganze was, at that time, a powerful independent kingdom and one of the most densely populated in that part of the continent. It was famed far and near for the abundance of its corn, rice, sugarcane and other agricultural products. Garenganze was also known for its copper mines, which were worked by the inhabitants. They cleansed and smelted the copper out of the ore with remarkable skill.

On reaching the capital, Arnot expected to have an early interview with the king. But it was not Msidi's habit to welcome strangers all at once. For some time Arnot was placed in a sort of quarantine while various tests were employed by witch doctors and diviners to see whether his intentions were good or bad and "whether his heart was as white as his skin." A little piece of bark, for instance, was placed at night in a certain liquid solution. If next morning the bark appeared quite sound, that showed that the heart of the newcomer was equally so. If, on the other hand, it was in the least decomposed, the inference was that his heart was rotten and that he must not be trusted.

Fortunately, after several days had been spent in experiments of this kind, everything turned out in Arnot's favor and the king accorded him a public reception that was both friendly and imposing. King Msidi, an elderly man with a white beard, folded his arms around the traveler in the most fatherly manner and then introduced him to his wives, of whom he had 500, as well as to his numerous brothers, cousins and other relatives. He invited Arnot to remain in Garenganze and to build himself a house on any site he pleased. This was the beginning of the Garenganze Mission.

A LONELY OUTPOST

For two years Arnot toiled on in that remote land, making tours of exploration from the capital into the surrounding districts. In most places, the people had never seen a white man before and his appearance created a great sensation. The very print of his boots on the path was a curiosity. "His feet," people said, "are not a man's feet; they are the feet of a zebra."

The oppression of Arnot's loneliness was increased by the vices and cruelties which went on in Garenganze. All around him the horrors of the slave trade prevailed. Infants born to enslaved women were constantly put to death because their owners had no use for them. The slave traders regarded them as positive nuisances, not only encumbering their mothers on the march, but also preventing them from carrying loads of ivory or some other commodity. As no one wanted to buy the helpless little creatures, the slavers quite commonly flung them into a river or dashed out their brains against the trunk of a tree.

The Trail of the Slave Traders

One day the body of a little boy was picked up on the road with a fatal spear gash through and through. It was a child whose owner shortly before had pressed Arnot to take it. Another infant whom he had felt unable to accept was thrown into the bush and devoured by wild beasts. And so, Arnot was led to resolve that he must at all costs save these poor slave children—a decision which soon brought him a large family of youngsters to whom he had to take the place of both father and mother.

Not less painful than the accompaniments of slavery was the prevalence of human sacrifice. King Msidi never entered upon any enterprise without seeking to ensure himself success by putting someone to death. No one knew beforehand who the victim might be. The king simply said that so-and-so was to be taken, and straightaway the appointed man or woman was led out to the slaughter.

Arnot held this missionary outpost for two years before re-inforcements arrived, and during all that time he never had a chance of receiving even a letter from the outer world. There is a heroism of patient endurance and continuance as well as a heroism of bold achievement. It sometimes needs more courage to hold the trenches than to lead the forlorn charge. Arnot showed himself a hero in both kinds.

•••

Source Material. Mr. Arnot's book, from which the above sketch is drawn, is entitled *Garenganze, or Seven Years' Pioneer Mission Work in Central Africa* (London: James E. Hawkins, 1889).

ADVOCATES
FOR THE ISLANDS

Like James Evans and Fred Arnot, Coley Patteson and James Calvert responded to direct invitations, but not from the people they would minister to. Patteson was recruited by the bishop of New Zealand, half in jest, at the age of 14. The Calverts' ministry in Fiji was initiated by the king of Tonga, who had seen the transformative power of the gospel among his own people and wanted his neighbors to hear the same message. Those who follow Jesus long to see others know Him too. In some cases, this takes them on long journeys and through wild adventures. But it may also mean moving others to take those journeys and have those adventures. Responding to the bishop's invitation eventually cost Coley Patteson his life. James Calvert lived to see the fruit of his efforts in Fiji.

PART III

ADVOCATES
FOR THE ISLANDS

CHAPTER 5

THE MAN WHO DIDN'T LOOK LIKE A MURDERER

JOHN PATTESON IN MELANESIA

A BISHOP'S INVITATION

JOHN COLERIDGE PATTESON, or Coley, as he was familiarly called, was the son of a distinguished British lawyer and the grandnephew of the poet Coleridge. As a boy, Coley was especially known for his physical prowess, which raised him ultimately to the coveted position of captain of the Eton cricket team. But this brilliant cricketer had other qualities which do not always accompany athletic distinction. He was a quick and diligent scholar, especially strong in languages. This fact stood him in good stead when he came to move about in a scattered archipelago, almost every island of which had its own separate dialect. Better still, he was a lad of fearless moral courage. While up to any amount of fun, he could not tolerate any kind of coarseness or indecency.

It was while Coley was at Eton, at about 14 years of age, that a vision of what was to be the great work of his life first dawned upon him. In the parish church of Windsor one Sunday afternoon, he heard a missionary sermon from Bishop Selwyn of New Zealand, a diocese which at that time included the Melanesian Islands. Coley was deeply touched by the bishop's appeal for help. Not long afterward, he met Bishop Selwyn face to face. The bishop, who was just about to leave England for the South Seas, turned to the boy's mother and said, half in playfulness, half in earnest, "Lady Patteson, will you give me Coley?" From that day forward, deep down in the heart of the lad there lived the thought of someday joining the pioneer work among the islanders of the Pacific.

Bishop Selwyn's Plan

When the see[11] of New Zealand was first formed, Bishop Selwyn was entrusted with the care of the innumerable islands dispersed in various groups over the South Pacific. The interest of the Church of England in the islanders, however, had been anticipated by the zeal of other churches and missionary societies. The Wesleyans were at work in the Fiji Islands, the Presbyterians in the New Hebrides, the London Missionary Society in Polynesia. There still remained farther to the west, and forming a far-off fringe along the southeastern coast of New Guinea and the northeastern coast of Australia, the Melanesian group. Bishop Selwyn very wisely resolved that, to prevent overlapping of missionary effort and consequent confusion, he would confine his attentions to these Melanesians.

He entered into his labors among them with all the ardor and heroism of the true pioneer. Like his future colleague Coleridge Patteson, Selwyn was a distinguished athlete. He had rowed in the first InterUniversity Boat Race in 1829 and was further a splendid pedestrian and a magnificent swimmer. In his work in Melanesia, all these powers came into full play.

There was nothing of the conventional bishop about Selwyn's outward appearance or manner of life. His usual way of landing on an island was to dive headfirst from a boat which lay off at a safe distance and swim ashore through the surf. When hard manual work had to be done, he was the first to set the example. If dangers had to be met, he did not hesitate to face them. If hardships had to be borne, he bore them cheerfully. Once, for instance, when an inhospitable chief refused him the shelter of a hut, he retired to a pigsty and spent the night there, patient and content.

---

11. In the Church of England, a see is the geographical jurisdiction of a bishop.

How versatile Bishop Selwyn was may be judged from an instance like the following. On one occasion, he had undertaken by request to convey to New Zealand in his missionary schooner a Melanesian chief's daughter and her attendant. The pair were dressed according to the ideas of propriety which prevailed in the islands, but were hardly presentable in a British colony. The bishop spent much of his time on the voyage in manufacturing, to the best of his ability, two petticoats out of his own bedspread. And so attractive did he make the garments, with their trimmings of scarlet ribbon, that the Melanesian girls were as delighted to put them on as the bishop was anxious that they should do so.

One of the great difficulties of the work in Melanesia sprang from the endless varieties of dialects which were employed. Bishop Selwyn conceived the plan of persuading youths from the different islands to come with him to New Zealand to undergo there a course of instruction and training which would fit them for Christian work among their own people when they returned, effectively multiplying his missionary efforts. But if this plan was to be carried out efficiently, there was need of assistance, and such assistance as was required was by no means easy to find. The man wanted must be possessed of physical hardihood, ready and fit to "rough it" as the bishop himself did while cruising among the islands. But he must also be a man of culture and character, to whom the difficult task of educating the youths could be safely entrusted.

In search of such a helper as this, Bishop Selwyn eventually paid a visit to England. Thirteen years had passed since he had stirred the missionary instinct in young Patteson's soul by saying to his mother in his hearing, "Will you give me Coley?" Neither the bishop nor the boy had forgotten the incident. Coley, meanwhile, had graduated from Oxford and become curate of Alfington. His mother was dead, his father now an old man in poor health. A strong sense of filial love and duty had kept him from the thought of leaving home so long as his father was alive. Bishop Selwyn came to see the elder Patteson and Coley and set the claims of Melanesia before them in such a way that both father and son realized that they must not hesitate to make the needful sacrifice of affection. That sacrifice was soon made. When the bishop sailed again, Coleridge Patteson stood beside him on the deck as his devoted follower and brother missionary.

ROVING ABOUT

As Patteson knew that his work would largely consist in sailing about among the islands, he applied himself busily throughout the long ocean voyage not only to the task of mastering the native languages under the bishop's tutelage, but to a careful study under the captain of the art of navigation. He soon became an expert shipmaster so that he was able, by and by, to navigate the *Southern Cross*, the little missionary schooner, on her various voyages through dangerous seas.

Arriving in New Zealand, Patteson had a taste of the kind of life that was in store for him. His immediate work lay in the College which had been established for the island youths, but he had to be ready, just as Bishop Selwyn himself was, to turn his hand to any kind of duty. Patteson's special task was, as he put it himself, "to rove about the Melanesian department," and for several years he spent half of his time at sea. He took thorough delight in his work, enjoying its adventurous aspects, but still more feeling the privilege of carrying the gospel of Christ to men and women who had never heard it before and who needed it very badly.

On his early cruises, Patteson was accompanied by the bishop, and their most frequent method of landing at any island to which they came was to plunge into the sea and make for the crowd of armed natives who were sure to be standing on the beach. Sometimes they were in danger, but firmness and kindness and tact carried them through. In not a few cases they were able to persuade a chief to allow his son, or some other promising youth, to return with them to New Zealand to join the other young men who were receiving the elements of a Christian education.

So friendly was their reception, for the most part, that Patteson was inclined to scoff at the common European practice of describing these gentle-looking island people as savages. But at times, he was inclined to carry his confidence too far. It was well for him in those early days that he had Bishop Selwyn at hand, who had learned by experience the need for perpetual caution. At one island, they were received with every sign of friendliness and conducted to the chief's long hut. They saw hanging from the roof a row of human skulls, some of them black with soot, others so white that it was evident they had been quite lately added to the collection.

In another place, while passing through some bush, they came upon the remains of human bodies, relics of a recent cannibal feast. Occasionally, too, as they swam away from what had seemed to be a friendly crowd, an arrow or two whizzed past their heads, showing that they had left some ill-disposed persons behind them. One island that they visited in safety they knew to have been the scene some time before of a deed of blood of which the crew of a British vessel were the victims. Their ship had struck upon the reef, and when they got ashore the islanders killed the whole ship's company of them, 19 in all. Ten of these the cannibals ate on the spot. The remaining nine they sent away as presents to their friends.

BISHOP PATTESON

In 1861, after six years of strenuous apprenticeship to the work of a pioneer missionary in the Pacific, there came a great change in Coleridge Patteson's position. Bishop Selwyn had long been convinced of the necessity of forming Melanesia into a separate diocese and had come to recognize not less clearly the preeminent fitness of Mr. Patteson to occupy the new see. Coley Patteson became Bishop of Melanesia at the early age of 33.

His elevation made little difference, however, either in the general character of his work or in his manner of doing it. He cruised about among the islands on the *Southern Cross* as before, dressed commonly in an old flannel shirt and trousers somewhat the worse for wear, a handy costume for one who had constantly to do a good deal of swimming and wading. His voyages as bishop, however, were on a wider scale than any he had attempted formerly, for he felt his larger responsibilities and tried to reach even those islands which had so far been regarded as inaccessible.

Several times Patteson had very narrow escapes. Once, in particular, when he had gone ashore at a place where the local people made a show of friendship, he discovered from their conversation and gestures that it was their deliberate intention to kill him. The reason, he found afterwards, was that one of their friends had been murdered by a white trader, and they felt that they were entitled to a white man's life. The bishop knew that, humanly speaking, he had no chance of mercy, but he begged permission to be allowed to pray. Kneeling down, he committed his soul to God. The islanders did not understand a single word that he uttered, but the look they saw in his face as he knelt so impressed and overawed them that they said to one another, "He does not look like a murderer." As soon as Patteson finished praying, they courteously conducted him back to the beach and bade him farewell.

A Rudder for a Shield

On another occasion, a sad incident took place at the island of Santa Cruz. The Melanesians here showed no signs of opposition when he landed, but after he had returned to his boat and pushed off, a shower of arrows was discharged from the beach. Bishop Patteson, who was at the stern, unshipped the rudder and held it up as a shield to try to ward off the deadly shafts. In spite of his efforts, three of the party, all of them Christian young men, were transfixed. Fortunately, the arrows were not poisoned, as Melanesian arrows often were, but Patteson had great difficulty in extracting them. He found it quite impossible to draw out the arrowhead from one man's wrist and was obliged to pull it from the other side right through his arm. This poor fellow contracted lockjaw[12] and died in a few days, after dreadful agonies of pain.

A Shadow Falls

For 10 strenuous years, Bishop Patteson sailed to and fro among the Melanesian Islands. Sometimes, through illness and weakness brought on by the constant strain, he was in great suffering, but he never ceased to rejoice in his work. At last, however, a dark shadow fell across his path, a shadow which deepened to the awful tragedy of his death.

The traders of the Pacific had discovered that it was more profitable to kidnap Melanesian people, lock them under hatches and sail with them as virtual slaves to the plantations of Queensland or Fiji, than to busy themselves in collecting sandalwood or copra[13] for the legitimate market. Not a few Europeans had entered into this unscrupulous and vile traffic, which soon produced an unpleasant change all over the islands in the attitude of the local people to foreigners.

Worse still, some of these kidnappers used Bishop Patteson's name as a decoy. Coming to an island where he was known and trusted, they would tell the people that the bishop was on board and wanted to see them. When the unsuspecting islanders came out in their canoes and climbed on board, they were quickly imprisoned in the hold. These were the malign influences which led to the murder of Bishop Patteson. It was the kidnapping traders more than the ill-used Melanesians who were responsible for his death.

In September 1871, the *Southern Cross* stood off the coral reef of the island of Nukapu.[14] Several canoes were seen cruising about,

---

12. Tetanus.
13. Dried coconut kernels.
14. Now part of the Solomon Islands.

apparently in a state of some excitement. The bishop and part of his crew pulled toward the shore in a small boat, but the tide was too low to cross the reef. At this juncture, two islanders offered to take the bishop into their light canoe and paddle him over the reef to the shore. He at once consented. The boat's crew saw him land safely on the beach, but after that lost sight of him. About a half hour later, a shower of arrows fell upon them from several canoes, which had gradually been drawing near. The crew pulled back immediately in great haste and were soon out of range, but not before three persons had been struck with poisoned arrows, two of whom subsequently died.

When the tide rose high enough to make it possible for the boat to cross the barrier reef, it was dispatched again from the schooner in the hope of getting some news about Bishop Patteson. As the crew pulled across the lagoon toward the shore, two canoes put off to meet them. One cast off the other and went back. When the boat came near the canoe which had been left drifting, the crew noticed what looked like a bundle lying in the bottom. When they drew alongside, they saw that this was the dead bishop, lying there with a calm smile on his upturned face. On his chest lay a leaf of the coconut palm with five knots tied in the long sprays. What those mysterious knots meant was partly explained when the mat was unwrapped and five deadly wounds, inflicted with club, spear and arrows, were discovered on the body.

It was afterwards learned that five Nukapu natives had been stolen by white kidnappers. The islanders looked upon them as having been murdered. Their nearest relatives, exercising the old tribal right of exacting blood for blood, had stained their weapons one by one in the blood of the bishop, who was thus called upon to lay down his life for the sins of his unworthy fellow countrymen.

The people of Nukapu have long since repented of the bishop's killing. On the spot where he fell there now stands, by their own desire, a simple but impressive cross with this inscription upon it:

In memory of
John Coleridge Patteson
Missionary Bishop
Whose life was here taken by men for whom he would gladly have given it.

•••

Source Material. The authoritative source for Bishop Selwyn's life is the biography by Rev. H. W. Tucker (London: William Wells Gardner, 1879) and for Bishop Patteson's, *The Life of John Coleridge Patteson*, by Miss C. M. Yonge (London: Macmillan and Co., 1874). Mention should also be made of *Bishop Patteson*, by J. Page (London: S. W. Partridge and Co., [1911?]), which is an excellent popular narrative.

CHAPTER 6

FROM THE KING OF TONGA WITH LOVE

JAMES AND MARY CALVERT IN FIJI

A KING'S COMMISSION

ALMOST DUE NORTH OF NEW ZEALAND, but at a distance of nearly 1,200 miles, lies a group of islands of surpassing loveliness. They are about 250 in number, ranging from the size of a large county to barren rocks which disappear altogether at the highest tides. To the invariable beauty of all volcanic islands in the tropics, this group adds the peculiar charms of the coral formations of the Pacific. Mountains clothed in the most luxuriant vegetation toss their fretted peaks high into the air. Great green breakers dash perpetually on the barrier reefs, sending their snowy foam up to the very roots of the coconut trees that fringe the long shining beaches. Inside of the reefs, the lagoon lies sleeping, indigo blue where its waters are deepest, emerald green nearer to the shore, but always of such crystal clearness that the idle occupant of a canoe can see, far down at the bottom, the white sands, the richly tinted seaweeds and the exquisite coral growths branching into innumerable varieties of form and blossoming with all the colors of the rainbow. These are the Fiji Islands.

In these fair islands, however, one might say the air was always tainted with the smell of blood. Even among the violent peoples of the South Seas, the Fijians were notorious for every kind of brutality. Man eating was not only practiced, but gloried in and gloated over. Woe to the unfortunate crew whose ship drifted onto the reefs of a Fiji island! If they escaped from the cruel breakers, it was only to be dispatched by a club as soon as they reached the shore and then cooked forthwith in a huge cannibal oven.

Cannibalism was only one of the many forms of Fijian cruelty, for without the sacrifice of human blood nothing of importance could be undertaken. If a war canoe was to be launched, it was dragged down to the water over the prostrate bodies of living men and women, who were always mangled and often crushed to death in the process. When a chief's house was being built, deep holes were dug for the wooden pillars on which the house was to rest. A man was thrown into each hole, and he was compelled to stand clasping the pillar with his arms while the earth was filled in right over his head.

At the death of a Fijian of any consequence, his wives were strangled and buried beside him to furnish what was called "lining for his grave." His mother, if still alive, suffered the same fate. It was the eldest son's duty, when his father died, to take the leading part in the strangling of both his mother and grandmother. The lives of more distant female relatives and connections were spared, but they had to express their grief by sawing off one of their fingers with a sharp shell, joint by joint, so that it was hardly possible to find a woman in the islands who had not suffered mutilation in both her hands.

Despite their cruelty, however, the Fijians' social laws were elaborate. As manufacturers of cloth, and especially of pottery, they were famous far and wide in the Pacific. Canoes came hundreds of miles from other island groups to purchase their wares. They also enjoyed a unique reputation as wigmakers and hairdressers. Every chief had his own private hair artist, who spent hours each day over his master's head.

It was between the 1830s and 1840s that the first pioneers of Christianity came to Fiji. About 250 miles to the east lie the Friendly Islands,[15] inhabited by a people called Tongans. In the Friendly Islands the Wesleyan missionaries had met with remarkable success. The Tongans nearly all became Christians, including their king. As an unbeliever, this man had been a famous fighter,

---

15. Tonga.

leading out his war canoes and spreading death and devastation far and near. Now that he was a Christian, the king of Tonga was no less zealous in seeking to spread the gospel of peace. Both he and his people were especially eager that Christianity should be carried to Fiji, and they persuaded the Wesleyans to make the attempt. The Rev. James Calvert and his wife, Mary, were among the pioneers in this dangerous enterprise. Mr. Calvert was the only one who was spared to see the marvelous transformation which passed over the archipelago within the course of a single generation, and can only be compared to the transition that takes place within a single hour in those same tropical regions from the darkness of the night to the glory of the morning.

A KING'S CRUELTY

On the island of Bau, which lies near the heart of Fiji, there lived at that time an old king called Tanoa, one of the most ferocious of maneaters, and his son Thakombau, a prince of almost gigantic size and at the same time of unusual intelligence and character. Both the king of Bau and his son were celebrated warriors. In case of need, they could summon to their banner many scores of war canoes and their power to strike was felt all over Fiji.

Thakombau was capable of mildness, but with Tanoa, bloodthirstiness had become a kind of mania. Once, a near kinsman offended him, and though the culprit begged his pardon most humbly, Tanoa responded by cutting off the arm of the poor wretch at the elbow and drinking his warm blood as it flowed. Next, he cooked the arm and ate it in the presence of his victim, and then finally had him cut to pieces limb by limb. Tanoa was no more merciful to his own children than to those of other people, and on one occasion compelled one of his sons to club a younger brother to death.

With characteristic courage, the Wesleyan missionaries determined to strike at the very center of Fijian cruelty. They knew that if violence and evil could be cast down in Bau, the effects of its downfall would be felt in every island of the archipelago. On Bau itself Tanoa would by no means permit them to settle, nor would he allow any Christian services to be held on that island. He made no objections, however, to the Calverts building a house on an islet called Viwa, which is separated from Bau by only two miles of water, and he was quite willing to receive personal visits.

Mr. Calvert had many a conversation with the old king and his son. On Tanoa he made not the slightest impression, but over Thakombau he gradually gained an influence which was to lead, in due course, to the Christianization of the Fiji Islands. But it was Mary Calvert, not her husband, who gained the first victory in the fight.

Hospitality was a thing on which King Tanoa prided himself, and he never failed to entertain important guests with a banquet of human flesh. If enemies could be secured for the table, so much the better. If not, he had no hesitation in sacrificing his own subjects. On one occasion, a party of envoys from a pirate tribe had come to Bau to offer the king a share of their spoil by way of tribute. At once, a hunting party was sent out, which soon returned with 14 captives, all women—woman being considered an even greater delicacy than man. In those days, the fishing in Fiji was nearly all done by the gentler sex, and these unfortunates were wading in the sea with their nets when the hunters sighted them. Creeping up under the cover of a fringe of mangrove bushes which ran along the shore, Tanoa's men dashed suddenly into the water and seized the screaming women, who knew only too well what sort of fate awaited them.

Word of the occurrence came to the missionaries at Viwa almost immediately. Mr. Calvert was absent at the time on one of his numerous expeditions, but Mary and another lady who was with her resolved to do what they could to save the doomed women. They jumped into a canoe and paddled hastily across the strait. Before they reached the shore, the din of the death drums told them that the work of butchery had already begun. Every moment was precious now, and when they got to land, they took to their heels and ran toward the king's house.

By the laws of Bau, no woman was at liberty to cross King Tanoa's threshold on pain of her life, unless he sent for her. These two ladies thought nothing of their own danger. They rushed headlong into the king's presence and, with arms outstretched, besought him to spare the remaining victims. The very boldness of their action made it successful. Tanoa seemed quite dumbfounded by their audacity, but he at once ordered the work of slaughter to cease. Nine of the poor women had already been killed and carried off to the ovens, but the remaining five were immediately set at liberty.

THE KING'S DEATH

As King Tanoa was an old man whose end seemed to be drawing near, the prospect of his death and what might happen in connection with it gave the Calverts the deepest concern. They knew that if Fijian tradition was adhered to, the departure of so great a chieftain from the world was sure to be attended by a wholesale slaughter of his womenfolk. They also saw that if the practice could be broken down at Tanoa's funeral rites, a deadly blow would be struck at such abominations.

Mr. Calvert therefore visited Thakombau, the heir apparent, again and again, and urged him by every consideration in his power to abandon the idea of slaughtering his father's wives. He tried to appeal to Thakombau's better feelings. He promised to give him a very handsome present if he would refrain from blood. Calvert even went so far as to offer to cut off his own finger, after the Fijian fashion of mourning, if the women might be spared. But though Thakombau was evidently impressed by Mr. Calvert's pleadings, he would give no assurance. Calvert learned afterwards that Tanoa himself had been privately instructing his son all the while that his wives must on no account be kept from accompanying him on his journey into the unseen.

The old king's death took place rather suddenly in the end, and on this occasion too Mr. Calvert happened to be absent on duty to a distant island. It fell to a younger missionary, Mr. Watsford, to take action. As soon as he heard of the death, Watsford made for Bau with all possible haste. Within Tanoa's house, and in the very presence of the corpse, the work of massacre had begun. Two wives were lying dead and a third had been summoned when the missionary burst in. When Thakombau saw him enter he became greatly excited and, trembling from head to foot, he cried out, "What about it, Mr. Watsford?"

"Refrain, sir!" Mr. Watsford exclaimed, speaking with great difficulty, for his emotions almost overpowered him. "Refrain! That is plenty. Two are dead."

But though Thakombau was moved, he would not yield. "They are not many," he said, "only five. But for you missionaries, many more would have accompanied my father." The other three victims were brought in—newly bathed, anointed with oil, dressed in their best as if going to a joyous feast. And there, in the presence of the foreigner as he kept pleading for their lives, they were made to kneel down on the floor. A cord was fastened round each of their necks and was gradually drawn tighter and tighter until their lives were extinct.

A Kingdom's Redemption

Though King Thakombau had not the courage yet to defy the ancient traditions of his people, the influence of a higher teaching had been slowly telling upon him. The day-dawn in Fiji was about to begin. Soon after King Tanoa's funeral, a Bau chief died, and Mr. Calvert was able in this case to persuade Thakombau to forbid any sacrifice of the women of the house. The usual preparations for murder had already been made and the royal command gave great offence to many. The chief executioner flung down his strangling cord and exclaimed, "Then I suppose we are to die like anybody now!" But a great victory had been won for humanity and Christianity. A precedent against a brutal custom had been established, which thereafter made it much easier to rescue the proposed victims of cruelty.

The greatest triumph of all came in 1857. A vast crowd was summoned by the beating of the very death drums which had formerly rolled out their invitation to the islanders to be present at a cannibal feast. Before that crowd Thakombau, the king of Bau, renounced his past, proclaimed his faith and declared his intention to live henceforth as a follower of Christ.

To those who read the story afterwards, the heroism of a missionary's life often lies in the faith and courage and tenacity with which he faced toils and dangers, even though his endeavors did not result in great outward achievements. But there are other cases in which the daring of the missionary adventurer's life appears not only in the trials and difficulties he faces, but also in the wonderful victories he wins. James Calvert was one such happy missionary.

When the Calverts reached Fiji, one of their first tasks was to gather up and bury the skulls, hands and feet of 80 men and women who had been sacrificed at a single feast. Often, men and women bound with ropes were dragged past their door, going literally like oxen to the slaughter. The very air James Calvert breathed was foul at times with the sickening odor of roasting human flesh. But this same missionary who had seen Fiji in its midnight gloom was spared to see it in the light of the sun rising. Calvert lived to see 1,300 churches crowded Sunday after Sunday by devout congregations. And where once the stillness of the night had often been broken by the death shriek of a victim or the cannibal's exultant death song, he was spared to hear, as he passed along the village paths after dark had fallen, the voices of fathers, mothers and little children rising together from many a home in sweet evening hymns.

•••

Source Material. *Cannibals and Saints*, by James Calvert; *At Home in Fiji*, by Miss C. F. Gordon Cumming (London: William Blackwood and Sons, 1901); *James Calvert*, by R. Vernon (London: S. W. Partridge and Co., 1890).

PART IV

FROM THE OUTSIDE IN

Allen Gardiner and Annie Taylor set their sights on two vastly different regions of the world. Mr. Gardiner dedicated his life to reaching the tribes of Tierra del Fuego, considered by most Europeans to be unapproachable and barely human. Miss Taylor was determined to trek into Lhasa, the forbidden city at the heart of Tibet. The methods Gardiner and Taylor adopted differed dramatically as well, but both displayed the same doggedness of purpose that overcame three failed attempts (each) to establish themselves among the communities they wanted to reach. They both eventually settled on a strategy of working from the fringes of their focus people. Despite the differences in their backgrounds, methods and experiences, both of these pioneers demonstrated a willingness to try, fail, learn, adjust and try again that is still essential for missionary service in hard places today.

CHAPTER 7

THE SHORES OF THE LAND OF FIRE

ALLEN GARDINER IN TIERRA DEL FUEGO

A PREPOSTEROUS IDEA

THE LARGE ARCHIPELAGO OF CLOSELY huddled islands which projects from Patagonia toward the Antarctic Ocean is known by the rather inappropriate name of Tierra del Fuego, or "Land of Fire." In the 1800s, the inaccessibility and desolation of the region, and the ferocious and almost inhuman reputation of the tribes encountered by vessels passing through the Straits of Magellan, made any thoughts of carrying the Christian gospel to this part of the world seem absolutely preposterous.

Charles Darwin visited the Magellan Straits on the *Beagle* and recorded his conviction that "in this extreme part of South America man exists in a lower state of improvement than in any other part of the world... One can hardly make oneself believe that they are fellow-creatures and inhabitants of the same world."

Travelers reported that the Fuegians had stunted figures, repulsive faces, a low grade of intelligence and an apparent lack of natural affection, as shown by the readiness of parents to throw their children overboard in a storm in order to lighten a canoe, or of children to eat their own parents when they had grown old and useless. Of Fuegian speech, Darwin wrote, "The language of these people, according to our notions, scarcely deserves to be called articulate." And yet, through the enterprise begun and inspired by the heroic man of whom we have now to tell, the sounds of the Fuegian speech were made to convey the story of the gospel, while the Fuegians themselves were changed from cannibals and thieves into peaceful, honest and industrious members of a Christian community.

A First Attempt

Allen Gardiner was a captain of the British Navy. When about 40 years of age, however, he determined to give up his chosen profession and devote the rest of his life to work among the unreached. It was toward South America that his steps were eventually guided. In Cape Horn, Gardiner chartered a crazy old schooner, the owners of which regarded her as no longer fit to go to sea, and succeeded in reaching the Straits of Magellan in March 1842.

Gardiner had provided himself with a few stores and planned to settle on one of the islands and try to win the confidence of the inhabitants. How difficult this task would be he soon discovered. Wherever he landed, whether on the islands or on the Patagonian coast, the Fuegians showed themselves so unfriendly that he realized the impossibility of making any headway without help and more adequate equipment. He resolved accordingly to return to England without delay and try to persuade one of the great missionary societies to take Patagonia and Tierra del Fuego under its care.

A Second Attempt

Unfortunately, not one of the existing societies was in a position at that time to undertake any fresh responsibilities. Captain Gardiner, nothing daunted, next made his appeal to the Christian public and succeeded at last in originating the South American Missionary Society. Gardiner and his assistant, Mr. Hunt, were eventually landed with their stores on the south coast of Patagonia and there left to their own devices.

For a time, they could see nothing of any locals, though they lighted fires in the hope of attracting notice. Eventually, they received some troublesome visitors in the persons of a chief whose name was Wissale, his wives and children and a party of followers.

Wissale, who had picked up a few words of English from passing ships, soon began to make matters exceedingly uncomfortable for the two Englishmen. His intention apparently was to force his company upon them, especially at mealtimes, and compel them to put their scanty stores at his disposal. It was speedily evident to the two unfortunate philanthropists not only that their provisions would soon be eaten up, but that in the mood of Wissale and his men their lives were hanging by a very slender thread. In this state of matters, a passing ship seemed to be providentially sent. Captain Gardiner felt that he had no alternative but to confess himself defeated and once more to return to England.

A THIRD ATTEMPT

The members of the South American Society were much discouraged. Captain Gardiner, however, never for a moment lost heart. Having once again raised the necessary funds, Gardiner persuaded the Society to allow him to set out with five companions. Owing to his former connection with the Navy, one of Her Majesty's ships, the *Clymene,* was placed at his disposal. "Hope deferred, not lost," became the Society's motto.

The *Clymene* reached the Magellan Straits at a time when a hurricane of wind was blowing, accompanied by violent storms of sleet and hail. After suffering severely from exposure to the inclement weather, Captain Gardiner was able to select a spot for his proposed station to which he gave the name of Banner Cove.[16] The friendly warship, however, had not yet proceeded on her voyage when a band of Fuegians came down on the little party encamped on the shore in so hostile and threatening an attitude that Gardiner felt that he must decide immediately whether it would be right to remain in this situation without any possible means of escape in the event of an attack. He had only a few hours in which to make up his mind, and the conclusion he came to was that he had no right to run the risk of sacrificing the lives of his five companions.

---

16. From Psalm 60:4: "But for those who fear you, you have raised a banner to be unfurled against the bow" (NIV).

Gardiner now began to realize that the only way in which he could hope to evangelize Fuegia was by having a vessel of his own, on board of which he might live when necessary, and be free at the same time to move about among the islands. Accordingly, he reembarked with his party on the *Clymene* and made his way homeward via Panama and the West Indies.

GARDINER'S FINAL ATTEMPT

Though his new idea filled Captain Gardiner with fresh enthusiasm, his enthusiasm was not widely shared. At this we can hardly wonder. Some of the Captain's best friends advised him to give the whole thing up. "Only with my life," was his reply. After Gardiner unsuccessfully sought financial support in England, Germany and Scotland, a lady in Cheltenham came forward with a generous donation. The result was that a party of seven was made up, including Captain Gardiner, and two strong double-decked boats were provided.

Having taken passage from Liverpool in the *Ocean Queen*, Captain Gardiner and his companions, with their stores and boats, were landed in Banner Cove on December 17, 1850. Gardiner sent a letter by the *Ocean Queen*, which left the next day for California, saying, "Nothing can exceed the cheerful endurance and unanimity of the whole party. I feel that the Lord is with us, and cannot doubt that He will own and bless the work which He has permitted us to begin." From that point all communication with the outer world absolutely ceased.

We must now follow the story as it was later revealed in Captain Gardiner's diary. The party landed with some difficulty, owing to a sudden gale which sprang up before the *Ocean Queen* was out of sight. Not long after, the Fuegians made their appearance. Several war canoes gathered in the bay, the men on board being all armed with spears, and it was clear from their demeanor that they were only waiting for a suitable opportunity to make a sudden and overwhelming rush. Gardiner accordingly resolved, with great reluctance, to leave Banner Cove and sail to another inlet known as Spaniard Harbor.

A few days after their arrival in that place, one of those violent hurricanes sprang up for which the region all around Cape

Horn was notorious. The boats were torn from their anchorage and dashed ashore. Troubles now began to thicken. Scurvy broke out—a deadly disease for men in such a situation—and not long after, provisions began to run short. Now and then, a few fish were caught or an occasional wild fowl was knocked over on the beach, but no reliance could be put upon these sources of support. The remaining months were months of dreadful suffering. It had now become evident that food might utterly fail before any relief came. The outlook was dark indeed.

Attack Looms

THE RESCUE ATTEMPT

And now something must be said of the search for Captain Gardiner and its results. The Society had unexpected difficulty shipping supplies from England to Tierra del Fuego. They therefore hastily commissioned a schooner in a South American port, under Captain W. H. Smyley, to locate Captain Gardiner. Smyley arrived at Banner Cove on October 21, 1851. No one was to be seen, but on the rocks at the entrance to the cove the words were painted,

GO TO SPANIARD HARBOUR
MARCH 1851

Following these directions, Captain Smyley sailed to the place indicated, where, in his own words, he saw a sight that was "awful in the extreme."

In a stranded boat on the beach, a dead body was lying. Not far off was another washed to pieces by the waves. A third lay half buried in a shallow grave. Rocks were later found painted with Psalm 62:5-8[17] and directions to a cave where another body lay. The remains of Captain Gardiner were discovered by the side of a boat, from which he seemed to have climbed out and been unable to get in again. Gardiner's journal was also recovered, carefully written up to the last and giving many touching details of those dreadful months of starvation, disease and slowly approaching death.

Allen Gardiner's life is apt to strike us at first as one that was no less tragic in the fruitlessness of its great purpose than in the misery of its end. But it was not in vain that he and his brave comrades laid down their lives for Tierra del Fuego. The story of Captain Gardiner's death stirred England as he had never been able to stir her during his strenuous life. It helped to bring about in due course, through the heroic labors of other noble men who took up the unfinished task, that complete transformation of the Fuegians to which reference was made in the beginning of this chapter.

LAST WILL AND STRATEGY

Not long before his death, Captain Gardiner drew up a plan for the future of the work to which he had devoted his life. Experience had shown him a better way of attacking the problem of how to reach the inhabitants of Tierra del Fuego. The headquarters of the Mission should be transferred to one of the Falkland Islands, a lonely British group lying in the South Atlantic. To this station, a few Fuegian volunteers could be taken in successive parties so that the missionaries might have the double opportunity of acquiring their language and introducing them to Christian truth.

---

17. Psalm 62:5-8: "Yes, my soul, find rest in God; my hope comes from him. Truly he is my rock and my salvation; he is my fortress, I will not be shaken. My salvation and my honor depend on God; he is my mighty rock, my refuge. Trust in him at all times, you people; pour out your hearts to him, for God is our refuge" (NIV).

When the news reached England of the dreadful calamity which had overtaken Captain Gardiner and his whole party, the general feeling was that the brave seaman's hopes and plans were now buried with him forever in his lonely grave. But it was not so. At a time when most of the supporters of the Society were crushed and dispirited, Rev. G. P. Despard uttered the noble words, "With God's help, the Mission shall be maintained." He aroused in many others a spirit of prayerful determination like his own, and before long Captain Gardiner's schemes began to be literally fulfilled.

A stout little schooner, fitly called the *Allen Gardiner,* sailed from Bristol in 1855 with a fresh staff of missionaries, including Mr. Allen W. Gardiner, the only son of the departed hero. Keppel Island, one of the West Falklands, was secured from the British Government as a mission station. To crown the brightening prospects, Mr. Despard himself offered his services as superintendent of the Mission and sailed with his family for the Falklands.

A SECOND FIRST ATTEMPT

A well-known Fuegian, who called himself Jemmy Button, had once been taken to visit England by a ship captain. He had picked up a little English, which he was always pleased to air before the sailors of any passing vessel. As Button's command of English promised to be useful, he was invited to come with his wife and children to Keppel Island for several months, and he agreed. On his next voyage to Tierra del Fuego, Mr. Despard took Jemmy Button, according to promise, back to the familiar life of the wigwam and the canoe. He had no difficulty in persuading three other Fuegian families (including a lad named Okokko) to return with him to the Falklands.

Mr. Despard thought therefore that the first steps should now be taken toward establishing a missionary station in Tierra del Fuego itself. He resolved to make a start at Woollya, the neighborhood from which all his visitors had come. The enterprise was put into the hands of Mr. Phillips, one of the most trusted of the staff, and the *Allen Gardiner* sailed from Keppel Island for Woollya in October 1859. Week after week passed, and there was no sign of the returning vessel. At length, Mr. Despard grew so anxious that he engaged Captain Smyley to sail at once on a voyage of inquiry. It was not long before Captain Smyley once again returned with terrible news. The people of Woollya had massacred Mr. Phillips and seven others. Of the whole company on board the *Allen Gardiner*, only one had escaped.

The *Allen Gardiner* had been ransacked and plundered, but not otherwise destroyed. Captain Smyley was able to convey her back to the Falkland Islands in safety. He brought along with him Okokko and his wife, Camilenna, who begged to be removed from their violent surroundings and taken back once more to their Christian friends at Keppel Island.

The next voyage of the *Allen Gardiner* was to England, to which Mr. Despard now returned, leaving two missionaries to hold the fort in Keppel Island until better days should come. One of these was William Bartlett, the other Mr. Bridges, Mr. Despard's adopted son, a young man of a very fine spirit and possessed of a rare faculty for language. To him, more than to any other, the missionaries owed their eventual mastery of the difficult Fuegian tongue. In the care of the Mission property, in the further instruction of Okokko and Camilenna and in the task of learning not only to speak Fuegian, but how to reduce it to a grammar, these two brave men whiled away the lonely months and years of waiting.

STARTING AGAIN

After two such crushing blows as had now fallen upon the South American Society within the space of eight years, it might almost be supposed that any idea of converting the Fuegians would be finally abandoned. But the patient heroism of the founder had become part of the Society's inheritance and there was no slackening in the determination to go on. In 1862, the *Allen Gardiner* sailed from Bristol once again with a fresh missionary party to resume her work in the icy southern seas. The leader of the enterprise on this occasion was Mr. Waite Stirling. He was greatly assisted by both Mr. Bridges and Okokko, for the former had now become quite an expert in Fuegian, while the latter could speak English very well. As the schooner sailed about among the islands, the missionaries, by means of these two highly competent interpreters, made their friendly intentions everywhere known.

At Woollya, they were received with some suspicion, for the

people there, recognizing the vessel, thought not unnaturally that it had come back now on a mission of vengeance. But when persuaded that their crime had been forgiven, they became quite enthusiastic, and far more of them volunteered to come to Keppel Island than could possibly be accommodated there. Year after year, the *Allen Gardiner* continued to go forth on her blessed work, bringing successive batches of Fuegians to Keppel and taking them home again after a while to act the part of the leaven in the midst of the meal. At last, in 1869, a mission station was opened at Ushuaia, some distance to the west of Spaniard Harbor.

A genuine reformation in the Fuegian character had now begun. The violent peoples of the Archipelago were being transformed into the likeness of peaceable Christian men and women. Proof of this is found in a British Admiralty chart of 1871. In this chart, the attention of mariners passing through the Straits of Magellan is directed to the existence of the mission station of Ushuaia. They are assured that, within a radius of 30 miles, no shipwrecked crew need expect other than kindly treatment from any local people into whose hands they may fall.

Charles Darwin learned of the extraordinary difference which a few years had made in the habits of the Fuegians, whom he had once been inclined to regard as possibly furnishing a missing link between the monkey and the man. He confessed his astonishment, writing, "I could not have believed that all the missionaries in the world could ever have made the Fuegians honest." Though not by any means a professing Christian, nor an advocate in general of Christian missions, he became from that time a regular donor to the funds of the Society which Allen Gardiner founded, which was "about as emphatic an answer to the detractors of missions," *The Spectator*[18] once remarked, "as can well be imagined."

•••

Source Material. *Hope Deferred, Not Lost*, by the Rev. G. P. Despard (London: Seeleys, ca. 1852); *From Cape Horn to Panama*, by Robert Young (London: South American Mission Society, 1900); *Captain Allen Gardiner: Sailor and Saint*, by Jesse Page (London: S. W. Partridge and Co., 1897); *Journal of Researches during the Voyage*

---

18. A popular British news and opinion magazine.

of H.M.S. Beagle, by Charles Darwin (London: John Murray, 1845). The author is indebted to *The Story of Commander Allen Gardiner, R.N.,* by the Rev. John W. Marsh and the Rev. W. H. Stirling (London: James Nisbet and Co., 1867) and also to Mr. Marsh's *First Fruits of the South American Mission* (London: William Macintosh, 1873), which was kindly lent him by the Secretaries of the Society.

CHAPTER 8

THE EDGE OF THE ROOF OF THE WORLD

ANNIE TAYLOR IN TIBET

A PREPOSTEROUS IDEA

IN THE 1800S, A SENSE of mystery shrouded Lhasa, the city of the Grand Lama, which wrapped itself in a veil of cold aloofness from European eyes. Prior to 1904, only one Englishman, Thomas Manning, had succeeded in reaching Lhasa. Two French missionary priests, the Abbes Hue and Gabet, undertook the journey, and though they reached their goal, they gained little by it, for they were soon deported back to China again.[19] Until the 20th century, no Protestant missionary ever set foot in Lhasa. What is more, no Protestant missionary, with one exception, ever made a determined attempt to reach it. The one who made the attempt (and all but succeeded) was a British lady.

Miss Annie Taylor went out to China in 1884 in the service of the China Inland Mission. She worked for some time at Tau-chau, a city which lay in the extreme northwest and quite near the Tibetan frontier. In 1887, she paid a visit to the great lama monastery of Kum-bum, the very monastery in which MM Hue and Gabet had stayed long before while they were learning the Tibetan language. The memory of these two adventurous priests

---

19. Catholic missionaries Evariste Regis Huc and Joseph Gabet disguised themselves as Buddhist monks to travel in this region.

may have stirred a spirit of imitation in a kindred heart. What chiefly pressed upon Miss Taylor's thoughts as she stood in the Kum-bum lamasery and looked out to the west was the vision of that great unreached land which stretched beyond the horizon for a thousand miles.

That this land was not only shut, but almost hermetically sealed against foreigners she knew perfectly well. But her dictionary did not contain the word "impossible." She recalled Christ's marching orders to His Church, "Go ye into all the world!" and said to herself, "Our Lord has given us no commands which are impossible to be carried out." And if no one else was ready in Christ's name to try to scale "the roof of the world" and press on into the sacred city of Lhasa itself, she determined that she, at all events, would make the attempt.

A FIRST ATTEMPT

Miss Taylor's first idea was to make India her point of departure. Lhasa lies much nearer to India than to China, though the comparative shortness of this route is balanced by the fact that it leads right over the Himalayas. She went accordingly to Darjeeling, pressed on into Sikkim and settled down near a Tibetan fort called Kambajong[20] with the view of mastering the language thoroughly before proceeding any farther.

From the first, the Tibetan suspicion of all strangers showed itself. Villagers would often ask her in an unpleasant manner what they should do with her body if she died. Her answer was that she had no intention of dying just then. The intentions of the natives, however, did not coincide with her own, and they next resorted to a custom of "praying people dead." Their faith in the power of prayer did not hinder them from giving heaven some assistance in getting their prayers answered. One day, the chief's wife invited Miss Taylor to dinner and set before her an appetizing dish of rice and eggs. She had not long partaken of it when she fell seriously ill with all the symptoms of aconite poisoning.

20. Sometimes spelled Khamber Jong or Kampa Dzong, now a town in Tibet.

A SECOND ATTEMPT

On her recovery, Miss Taylor wisely left Kambajong and settled down in a little hut near the Tibetan monastery of Podang Gumpa in Sikkim.[21] After a year spent in this way, for 10 months of which she never saw the face of another white person, Miss Taylor realized the impracticability of making her way to Lhasa by the Himalayan route. It was far more jealously guarded than the one from the frontiers of China. She decided, therefore, to return to China, and to make it her starting point. Her time in Sikkim had not been wasted. In the first place, she had not only learned Tibetan thoroughly, but had acquired it in its purest form as spoken at Lhasa. In the next place, she had gained a friend and attendant who was to prove of invaluable service to her in her future wanderings.

Tea with Pontso and His Wife

A young Tibetan named Pontso, a native of Lhasa, had met with a serious accident while traveling on the frontiers of India. Someone directed him to Miss Taylor for treatment. He had never seen a foreigner before, but the kindness and care with which she nursed him in his sufferings completely won his heart. He became a believer in the religion which prompted such goodness to

---

21. Now the Phodang or Phodong Monastery.

a stranger and devoted himself thenceforth to the service of his benefactress. Pontso soon justified the trust she placed in him by his unfailing courage and fidelity.

A THIRD ATTEMPT

Taking Pontso with her, Miss Taylor now sailed to Shanghai and made her way up the Yang-tse River for 2,000 miles. She settled again in Tau-chau on the Tibetan frontier, the city where she had begun her missionary service some seven years earlier. By way of preparing herself still further for her projected march into the interior, she visited a number of lamaseries in that region, made friends with the lamas and learned everything she could about the Tibetan religion and ways of life and thought.

About a year after her return to Tau-chau, the opportunity came for which she had been waiting. Among her acquaintances in the town was a Chinese man named Noga. He was a trader who had several times been to Lhasa, and on his last journey had brought away a Lhasa wife, Erminie. According to a Tibetan custom, he had married her only for a fixed term, and as the three years named in the bond were now fully up, Erminie was anxious to return to her native city and Noga quite willing to convey her back. The only question was one of ways and means. When they found that Miss Taylor wished to go to Lhasa, Noga made a proposal. He would himself guide her all the way to the capital, provided she supplied the horses and met all necessary expenses. Miss Taylor at once agreed to his terms, which, if he had been honest, would have been advantageous to both parties. But Noga was a deep-dyed scoundrel, as Miss Taylor soon discovered to her cost.

On September 2, 1892, Annie Taylor set out on her heroic enterprise accompanied by her faithful attendant Pontso, Noga and Erminie, a young Chinese man whom she hired as an additional assistant and a Tibetan frontiersman named Nobgey who asked permission to join the little company as he also was bound for Lhasa. There were 16 horses in the cavalcade, two mounts being provided for most of the travelers and several packhorses loaded with tents, bedding, cloth for barter, presents for chiefs and provisions for two months.

The little group had not proceeded far into the wild country when their troubles commenced. They came suddenly upon a group of eight bandits who were haunting the mountain track for the express purpose of relieving travelers of their valuables. Fortunately, the thieves had not noticed their approach and were seated round a fire enjoying the favorite Tibetan meal of tea. Moreover, the robbers were armed with old-fashioned matchlocks, the tinderboxes of which it took some time to light. As Miss Taylor's party was better armed, they succeeded in beating off their assailants.

Attacked by Bandits

Three days after, they overtook a caravan of friendly Mongols traveling in the same direction as themselves. In view of their recent experience, Miss Taylor and her companions thought it wise to combine forces with the Mongols. Their satisfaction at being thus reinforced was not long lived. Almost immediately, a band of robbers 200 strong swept down upon the caravan, entirely surrounded it and began firing from all sides. Two men were killed and seven wounded. Resistance was hopeless and the whole company had to surrender. The Mongols and Nobgey were robbed of everything and had to turn back, but the bandit code of honor forbids war upon women. Miss Taylor and her four companions were therefore allowed to pass on their way after being deprived of two of their horses and a good part of their luggage.

The next stage of the journey lay through the land of the Goloks. This fierce and warlike people had a great contempt for law and authority and acknowledged neither Tibetan nor Chinese rule. The chief delight of their lives was to engage in forays upon people of more peaceful tastes and habits than themselves. Issuing in large bodies from their mountain glens under some fighting chieftain, they swept down upon neighboring tribes and carried off as booty their cattle, horses, sheep, tents and other belongings. Among the Goloks, Miss Taylor would have fared even worse than she had already done at the hands of the bandits, but for the fact that the part of the tribe with which she first came in contact was ruled by a chieftainess. On discovering that this foreign traveler was also a woman, Wachu Bumo, the chieftainess, took quite a fancy to her. She not only saw to it that Miss Taylor was treated courteously so long as she remained in the Golok valleys, but insisted on furnishing her with an escort of two Golok horsemen to see her safely on her way for some distance after she had left the country of these marauders.

In England, Miss Taylor had been considered delicate, but a brave spirit and a strong will carried her through experiences which might well have broken down the strongest physique. For a great part of the journey to Lhasa, it must be remembered, the route ran among mountains covered with perpetual snow. Rivers had to be crossed which knew neither bridge nor ferry nor ford. Winter, too, was coming on, and they had often to advance in the teeth of blinding storms of sleet and snow. Shortly after they had left the land of the Goloks, the cold and exposure proved too much for Miss Taylor's Chinese companion, a tall, powerful young man. The travelers buried him as best they could in the frozen ground.

In a little mountain town called Gala, Miss Taylor made the interesting acquaintance of a couple, Pa-tegn and Per-ma, whose marriage had a flavor of romance unusual in Tibet. From infancy, Pa-tegn had been dedicated to the priesthood and had been brought up accordingly in a lamasery. But when about 20 years of age, he suddenly fell in love with Per-ma. The course of his true love could not possibly run smooth, for celibacy is binding on a Buddhist lama. But "one fine day," as Miss Taylor described it, "this Tibetan Abelard disappeared, and in company with Per-ma made his way to Lhasa." Here he discarded his priest's robe and became a tailor.

After a child had been born to them, Pa-tegn and Per-ma decided to return to Gala, and by means of a judicious present succeeded in soothing the outraged feelings of the local chief. In the house of this couple, Miss Taylor stayed for some time to rest from her fatigues. When she was setting out again, she persuaded Pa-tegn, who was an experienced traveler and knew Lhasa well, to come with her. It was fortunate for her that she secured his services. He proved a capable and devoted follower, and it would have gone ill with her, as she soon found out, but for his presence and help.

BETRAYAL

The travelers were now in the very heart of the mountains. Noga, their Chinese guide, feeling that Miss Taylor was thoroughly in his power, began to appear in his true character. It now became evident that his real purpose all along had been to rob and murder his employer before reaching Lhasa. More than once, he made deliberate attempts on her life, but on each occasion the vigilance of Pontso and Pa-tegn defeated his villainy. At last, he contented himself with deserting her altogether, carrying off at the same time, along with his wife, a horse, a mule and the larger of the two tents. The little party of three—Miss Taylor and the two loyal Tibetan men—was now reduced to such straits for lack of food that the remaining tent had to be bartered for the necessaries of life. Though it was now the middle of December in that awful climate, they had henceforth to sleep in the open air.

At length, the waters of the Bo-Chu River were crossed. The boundary of the sacred province of U,[22] in which Lhasa stands, and the goal of the journey seemed almost in sight. But alas for their hopes! In the middle of a deep gorge through which the path ran, two fully armed Tibetan soldiers sprang out from behind the rocks, ordered them to halt and took them prisoners. This was on January 3, 1893. Miss Taylor soon learned to what

---

22. Now known as U-Tsang.

this arrest was due. Noga, after deserting her, had hurried on in front for the purpose of lodging information that he had met two Tibetans conducting a European lady toward Lhasa. Guards were accordingly placed at all the approaches and Miss Taylor had walked into a prepared trap.

For several days, she was kept a prisoner surrounded by about 20 soldiers and having no better shelter by day or night than a narrow coffin-shaped hole in the ground. At last, she and her two attendants were brought before some chiefs who had been summoned from Lhasa. A trial was entered into which lasted for days, communication with the capital being kept up all the while by special messengers. Word came from Lhasa that the foreigner was to be treated courteously and this injunction was carefully attended to. But the issue of the trial was never in doubt. When only three days' march from the Sacred City, Miss Taylor, Pontso and Pa-tegn had to turn back and retrace every step of the weary way.

The return trip was even more trying than the advance, not only because hope was now turned to disappointment, but because winter in all its rigor now lay upon the land. The Tibetan authorities, though firm, were not unkind, and supplied Miss Taylor with provisions, some money and two horses. But the Tibetan climate made up for any gentleness on the part of the Lhasa chiefs. The cold was almost unspeakable. The food the three travelers tried to cook over their dung fires had often to be eaten half raw and little more than half warm, since at the great elevations of the mountain passes water boiled with very little heat. For 20 days at a stretch, they had to sleep on the ground in the open air, the snow falling around them all the while. They had no tent and there was no sign of any human habitation.

WORKING FROM THE FRINGE

Miss Taylor returned to China seven months and 10 days after she had set out for Lhasa. She made no further attempt to reach the Sacred City. That same year, 1893, was marked by the signing of the Sikkim-Tibet Convention. It designated the town of Yatung,[23] on the Tibetan side of the Indian frontier, open to all

---

23. Also spelled Yadong.

British subjects for the purposes of trade. In this political event Miss Taylor's discerning eye saw a missionary opportunity.

From China, she returned once more to the Himalayas and started a remarkable mission at Yatung. By and by, she secured the assistance of two other ladies—Miss Ferguson and Miss Foster. Nominally, Miss Taylor was a trader, this being the ground of her right to settle within the borders of the Forbidden Empire. In point of fact, she carried on some trade with the people of the district, who much preferred her dealings to those of the Chinese merchants and officials. But first of all, as both Chinese and Tibetans knew, she was a missionary, partly to the bodies (for her mission was provided with a medical dispensary), but above all to the souls of her beloved Tibetans.

Seldom surely in the annals of Christian missions has there been a more daring figure than that of Annie Taylor. She nearly succeeded in reaching Lhasa, but having failed, turned with a sanctified common sense to the open door offered by the trading regulations of the Sikkim-Tibet Convention. "The trading is not a hardship," she wrote. "If Paul could make tents for Christ, surely we can do this for our Master. So those who are 'called' to work for Tibet must be prepared for the present to sell goods to the Tibetans or attend to their ailments, as well as preach the gospel to them."

•••

Source Material. The story of Miss Taylor's march upon Lhasa, together with some account of her pioneer mission in the Chumbi Valley, can be found in her book, *Pioneering in Tibet* (London: Morgan and Scott, 1895).

VOLUNTARY CASTAWAYS

James Gilmour's story was once described this way: "Robinson Crusoe has turned missionary." Forced out of China by political unrest immediately after his arrival, Gilmour become an itinerant missionary to nomadic Mongols. He first immersed himself in traditional life and then traveled thousands of miles on foot and horseback between the Mongolian plains and Chinese trading centers. Joseph Neesima left his homeland of Japan by choice, but under penalty of death if discovered, because he wanted to learn about the outside world. In Boston he came across a secondhand copy of *Robinson Crusoe* and from it learned to pray to God as a "present, personal friend." Years later he returned to Japan, bringing the light of academic knowledge and spiritual truth that he had been willing to risk his life to find on foreign soil. Both men spent periods of their lives homeless and adrift, partially by choice, but that didn't stop them from making an eternal impact on the peoples they served.

PART V

VOLUNTARY
CASTAWAYS

CHAPTER 9

THE MISSIONARY TRAMP

JAMES GILMOUR IN MONGOLIA

FROM LONDON TO CHINA

ABOUT THE MIDDLE OF THE year 1870, there arrived in Peking[24] a young Scotchman, James Gilmour by name, who had been sent out to China by the London Missionary Society to begin work in the capital. Within a few weeks of his arrival, there took place at Tientsin,[25] the port of Peking, that violent outbreak known as the Tientsin massacre, in which a Roman Catholic convent was destroyed and 13 French people murdered. A widespread panic at once took hold of the capital. The European community felt that they were living on the edge of a volcano, for no one knew but that this massacre might be the prelude to a general outburst of antiforeign hatred.

All around, Gilmour's acquaintances were packing up their most precious belongings and holding themselves in readiness for a hurried flight to the south. It was at this moment that the newcomer resolved on a bold and original move. Instead of fleeing to the south in search of safety, he would turn his face northwards and see if an opening could be found for Christian work among the Mongols of the great Mongolian plains. Gilmour was utterly unacquainted both with the country and

---

24. Now Beijing.
25. Also known as Tianjin.

the language, but he had long felt a deep interest in that vast, lonely plateau which lies between China and Siberia. The suspension of work in Peking seemed to offer the very opportunity he wanted for pushing his way into Mongolia. And so as soon as the necessary preparations could be made, he left the capital behind with all its rumors and alarms. Before long, he passed the Great Wall, which ever since the third century BC had defended China from Mongolia. And then, with two camels and a camel cart, our intrepid traveler set his face toward the Gobi Desert, which lies in the very heart of the Mongolian plain.

FROM CHINA TO MONGOLIA

Mongolia is a huge plateau (1,800 miles from east to west and 1,000 miles from north to south) lifted high above the sea. It is part desert, part a treeless expanse of grassy steppe and in part covered by mountain ranges whose peaks rise up to the line of perpetual snow. The climate, hot and dry in summer and bitterly cold in winter, made agriculture impossible except in some favored spots. By the force of circumstances, the Mongols were nomads, dwelling in tents and pasturing flocks and herds upon the grass of the steppe.

About 500 years before Gilmour's arrival, the Mongols were converted to a form of Buddhism. This change of faith had a decidedly softening effect upon the national character. Much of this, no doubt, must be attributed to the custom which prevailed among them of devoting one or more sons in every family to the priesthood. One result of this custom was that the Mongol priests, or lamas as they were called, actually formed the majority of the male population. As the lamas were celibates by virtue of their office, another result was a great reduction in the population, as compared with earlier days. Mongolia no longer possessed the surplus swarms of bold and warlike horsemen which it once sent out to overrun and conquer other lands. But, like all nomads, its people were still an active and hardy race. As horsemen, too, they still excelled. It was to this country and this interesting but little-known people that James Gilmour devoted his life.

His first journey across the great plateau began northwest of

Peking, just within the Great Wall, and ended at Kiachta,[26] on the southern frontier of Siberia. He made this journey, which occupied only a month, in the company of a Russian official who knew no English, while he himself knew neither Russian nor Mongolian. He was glad, therefore, on reaching Kiachta to meet a fellow countryman, one of the world's ubiquitous Scots, in the person of a trader named Grant. Grant was exceedingly kind to Gilmour and took him into his own comfortable house. But finding that this contact with civilization was hindering him in his strenuous efforts to master the Mongolian language without delay, Gilmour formed a characteristic resolution. This was nothing else than to go out upon the plain and try to persuade some Mongolian to receive him as a guest.

It was at night that this idea occurred to Gilmour, and the next morning he left Kiachta, taking nothing with him but a heavy walking stick. Gilmour had already discovered that in Mongolia a strong stick was not only useful, but altogether indispensable, as a protection against the ferocious assaults of the wolfish-looking dogs which invariably rushed at a traveler if he drew near to any encampment.

As Gilmour approached a Mongol tent on the plains, he heard the sound of a monotonous voice engaged in some kind of chant. When he entered the tent, he found a lama at his prayers. The lama, hearing footsteps, looked round and pronounced the one word, "Sit!" and then continued his devotions. For another quarter of an hour, he went on, taking no further notice of his visitor meanwhile. But suddenly his droning chant ceased, and he came forward and gave Gilmour a hospitable welcome. Gilmour opened his mind to him without delay, telling him that it was his desire to spend the winter in his tent and learn Mongolian from his instruction. The lama was surprised, but perfectly willing, and agreed to receive his visitor as a paying guest. And so, within a few months of his departure from London, Gilmour was living the life of a nomad in the tent of a lama on the Mongolian plain.

_____

26. Also spelled Khyagt, Khyakhta, etc.

LIFE ON THE PLAINS

Once the first novelty had worn off, Gilmour found life somewhat monotonous. Dinner was the great event of the day, the more so as it was the only meal in which Mongols indulged. The preparations were unvarying, as was the menu. Toward sunset the lama's servant, who was a lama himself, would melt a block of ice in a huge pot over a fire which filled the tent with smoke. Taking a hatchet, he next hewed a solid lump of mutton from a frozen carcass and put it into the water. As soon as it was boiled, he fished it out with tongs and laid it on a board before his master and Gilmour, who attacked it with fingers and knives.

The typical Mongolian way of eating was to take a piece of meat in the left hand, seize it with the teeth and then cut off a mouthful close to the lips by a quick upward movement of a sharp knife. The operation looked dangerous, particularly for a European's comparably long and pointy nose. The Mongols always thought Gilmour's nose tremendous, and they excused him for cutting off his mouthfuls first and appropriating them afterwards.

Meanwhile, as this first course was in progress, the servant would throw some millet into the water used for boiling the meat. When the diners had partaken sufficiently of the solid fare, this thin gruel was served up as a kind of soup. The mutton, Gilmour said, was tough, but he declared that seldom in his life did he taste any food so delicious as this millet soup. He admitted that no doubt it was chiefly desert hunger that made it seem so good. Though he ate only once a day, the lama, like all Mongols, consumed vast quantities of tea. At dawn, and again at noon, the servant prepared a pailful of the cheering beverage, giving it always 10 or 15 minutes' hard boiling and seasoning it with fat and a little meal instead of milk.

Gilmour accommodated himself to the ways of the tent. As a concession to his Scotch tastes, however, he was provided every morning with a cupful of meal made into something like porridge by the addition of boiling water. This the lama and his servant called "Scotland," and they were careful to set it aside regularly for the use of "Our Gilmour," to whom, Buddhist priests though they were, they soon became quite attached.

When the time came at last to recross the plains to China,

Gilmour decided to make the homeward journey on horseback instead of by camel cart. The one drawback was that he had never yet learned to ride. But as he had found that the best way to learn Mongolian was by being compelled to speak it, he considered that a ride of a good many hundred miles might be the best way of learning to sit on a horse.

In Mongolia, a man who cannot ride was looked upon as a curiosity, and when Gilmour first mounted, everybody turned out to enjoy the sight of his awkwardness. But though he had one or two nasty falls, he soon learned to be quite at home on the back of his steed. When he rode once more through a gateway of the Great Wall, passing thus out of Mongolia into China again, he felt that after the training he had received on his way across the steppes and the desert, he would be ready henceforth to take to the saddle in any circumstances. Indeed, so sure of his seat had he become that on a subsequent occasion, when he formed one of a company mounted on Chinese mules traveling in single file, he sat backwards on his beast so as to be better able to engage in conversation with the rider who came behind him.

This crossing and recrossing of the Mongolian plain, and especially the winter he spent in the lama's tent, had already given Gilmour a knowledge of the Mongolian language and a familiarity with the habits and thoughts of the Mongols themselves such as hardly any other Westerner could pretend to. Peking, when he returned to it, had settled down to something like its normal quiet, but he felt that the ordinary routine of work in the city was not the work to which he was specially called. The desert air was in his blood now, and Mongolia was calling. Henceforth it was for the Mongols that he lived.

THE MISSIONARY TRAMP

Year by year Gilmour fared forth into the Great Plain in pursuit of his chosen task. Among the most remarkable of his many journeys was one which he made entirely on foot. He was a tremendous walker, more perhaps by reason of his unusual willpower than because of exceptional physical strength. On the occasion of his long tramp over the plains and back he had special reasons for adopting that method of locomotion. One was that grass was so scarce during that year that it would hardly have been possible to get pasture for a camel or a horse. Another was that the love of simplicity and unconventionality, which was so marked a feature of his character, grew stronger and stronger, and also the desire to get as near as possible to the poorest and humblest of the people.

In a Mongol Encampment

It was in keeping with his tastes, therefore, as well as from necessity, that Gilmour tramped through Mongolia with all his belongings on his back. His equipment when he set out consisted of a postman's brown bag on one side containing his kit and provisions. On the other side he carried an angler's waterproof bag with books, together with a sheepskin coat slung over his shoulder by means of a rough stick. The plainness of his garb may be judged of when we mention that, in one village on the border of China, he was turned out of the two respectable inns which the place could boast on the ground that he was a foot traveler without cart or animal who must be content to betake himself to the tavern for tramps. In the course of this journey, his formidable stick notwithstanding, Gilmour had sometimes to be rescued from the teeth of the dogs which flew, not unnaturally, at a character so suspicious looking. But he met with much hospitality from the people, both lamas and laymen, wherever he went, and he returned to China without any serious mishap.

From two dangers of the country Gilmour altogether escaped because he dressed as a Mongol. One was the risk of being attacked by wolves, which were a perfect terror to the Chinese traveler over the plains. The inhabitants themselves made light of the wolves and never hesitated when they caught sight of one to become the attacking party. The result of this was that the wolves were said to distinguish from afar between a Mongol and a Chinese. They slunk off as hastily as possible if they saw a wayfarer approaching in long skin robes but anticipated a good dinner at the sight of another in blue jacket and trousers.

The second danger Gilmour escaped was from bandits. For there were parts of the Gobi Desert, crossed as it was by the great trade routes between Siberia and China, which were quite as unpleasant to traverse as the ancient road between Jerusalem and Jericho. Gilmour's humble wardrobe made him unenticing to would-be thieves. He was probably never more secure against highway robbery than when he walked through Mongolia as a missionary tramp.

HEALING BODIES AND SOULS

Among the most interesting incidents which Gilmour recorded are some in connection with his endeavors to bring relief to those whom he found in sickness and pain. Although not a doctor by profession, he had picked up some medical and surgical skill and did not hesitate to use it on behalf of those for whom no better skill was available. He once undertook to treat a soldier for a bullet wound received in an encounter with brigands, thinking that it was only a flesh wound. It turned out to be a difficult bone complication. Gilmour knew hardly anything of anatomy, and he had absolutely no books to consult. "What could I do," he later recalled, "but pray?"

And a strange thing happened. There tottered up to Gilmour through the crowd an emaciated man whose bones stood out as distinctly as if he were a specimen in an anatomical museum, with only his skin drawn loosely over them. The man came to beg for cough medicine, but Gilmour was soon busy examining the part of his skeleton that was damaged in the other patient. The living model provided a way for Gilmour to learn, as he explained later, "what to do with the wounded soldier's damaged bone; and in a short time, his wound was in a fair way of healing."

Although it was Gilmour's custom to return to Peking for the winter, he continued while there to devote himself to his Mongol flock. Between China and Mongolia, a considerable trade was carried on, the Mongols bringing in hides, cheese, butter and the other products of a pastoral territory and carrying away in return vast quantities of cheap tea in the form of compressed bricks. These bricks were used in Gilmour's time not only for the preparation of the favorite beverage, but also as a means of exchange in lieu of money.

During the winter months, large numbers of traders arrived in Peking from all parts of Mongolia. Many of them camped out in their tents in open spaces, just as they did when living on the plains. Gilmour frequented these encampments and took every opportunity he could make or find of conversing about religious matters, and especially of seeking to commend "the Jesus doctrine," as the Buddhists called it.

One plan that he followed was to go about like a Chinese peddler, with two bags of books in the Mongolian language hanging from his shoulders. All were invited to buy, and in many cases this literature was taken up quite eagerly. Often a would-be purchaser demanded to have a book read aloud to him before he made up his mind about it. This gave the peddler a welcome chance of reading from the Gospels to the crowd which gathered and then of introducing a conversation about the merits of Jesus and Buddha. Sometimes those who were anxious to buy had no money but were prepared to pay in kind. And so, not infrequently, Gilmour was to be seen at night making his way back to his lodgings in the city "with a miscellaneous collection of cheese, sour curd, butter, millet cake, and sheep's fat, representing the produce of part of the day's sales."

James Gilmour's *Among the Mongols* is a book to be read, not only for the adventure of its subject matter, but because of the author's remarkable gift of realistic statement—his power of making his readers see things in bodily presence just as his own eyes had seen them. "Robinson Crusoe," wrote one reviewer, "has turned missionary, lived years in Mongolia, and written a book about it. That is this book."

•••

Source Material. *Among the Mongols,* by the Rev. James Gilmour (London: London Missionary Society, 1882) and *James Gilmour of Mongolia*, by Richard Lovett (London: Religious Tract Society, 1892); *The Far East*, by Archibald Little (Oxford: Clarendon Press, 1905).

CHAPTER 10

THE RETURN OF THE RUNAWAY SAMURAI

JOSEPH NEESIMA IN JAPAN

REJECTING WHITTLED THINGS

NEESIMA WAS BORN A JAPANESE samurai, a member of the old fighting caste of feudal times. He was 10 years old when Commodore Perry, of the U.S. Navy, steamed into the harbor of Uraga[27] and extorted from a reluctant government those treaties of friendship and commerce which broke down the walls of seclusion behind which Japan had long hidden herself from the eyes of the world.

As a boy, Neesima wore a samurai sword and was sworn to a life of fealty to the *daimio,* or prince, on whose estate he was born. From the first, however, it was evident that, despite being a lowly serf, he had a mind and will of his own and a passionate longing for truth and freedom. He devoted all his spare time to study, often sitting up over his books until the morning cocks began to crow. Once, the prince, his master, caught him running away from his ordinary duties to go to the house of a teacher whom he was in the habit of visiting by stealth. After giving the boy a severe flogging, the prince asked him where he was going. Neesima answered, "I wish to learn foreign knowledge." The *daimio* laughed at him, "You are a stable boy."

Not less remarkable than his thirst for knowledge was the lad's consciousness of the rights of human beings and passionate desire

---

27. The entrance to Tokyo Bay.

for fuller liberty. But above all, young Neesima felt a deep longing for God. When he was about 15 years of age, to the great distress of his relatives, he refused to worship any longer the family gods which stood on a shelf in the house. He saw for himself that they were "only whittled things" and that they never touched the food and drink which he offered to them. Not long after this, Neesima gained possession of an abridged Bible history in the Chinese language, with which he was well acquainted. He was immensely struck by the opening sentence, "In the beginning God created the heaven and the earth." Neesima immediately recognized the Creator's claim to be worshipped. To this still Unknown God he began thereafter to pray, "If You have eyes, look upon me; if You have ears, listen for me."

Japanese Girl Carrying Firewood Prays to Stone Images

LEAVING THE LAND OF THE RISING SUN

Before long, it became Neesima's constant desire to find his way to the port of Hakodate,[28] where he thought he might fall in with

---

28. On the southern tip of Hokkaido, Japan's northernmost island.

some Englishman or American from whom he could obtain the knowledge that he wanted. He made application to the *daimio* to be allowed to undertake the voyage, but got only a scolding and a beating for his pains. Yet he did not despair. He waited patiently for four or five years, and at last, to his inexpressible joy, secured permission to go to Hakodate in a sailing junk which belonged to his master. It was several weeks before he reached the haven of his hopes.

Arriving at Hakodate at last, it seemed for a time as if nothing but disappointment was in store for Neesima there. He could find no one to teach him English, and meanwhile his little stock of money melted rapidly away. At length, matters began to look brighter. He fell in with a Russian priest who gave him some employment and he made the acquaintance of a young clerk in an English store. That clerk not only taught Neesima a little English but helped to carry out the secret determination he had now formed of escaping to America.

Neesima had not come to this decision without long and anxious thought. It involved great sacrifices and no small danger. In those days, a Japanese subject was forbidden to leave the country on pain of death. If caught attempting to do so, he forfeited his life. If he made good his escape, he had banished himself forever from the "Land of the Rising Sun."

It was painful for Neesima to think of leaving his parents without even saying goodbye and with no prospect of ever seeing them again, especially as he had been brought up under the influence of the Confucian doctrine of filial obedience. But he thought the matter out and saw at last that in the search for truth and God it may be proper to set all other claims aside. "I discovered for the first time," he wrote afterward, "that the doctrines of Confucius on the filial relations are narrow and fallacious. I felt that I must take my own course. I must serve my Heavenly Father more than my earthly parents." After endless difficulties, Neesima's clerk friend secured leave for him to work his passage to Shanghai on an American schooner, the *Berlin*. He had, of course, to smuggle himself on board at his own risk with the full knowledge that if he was detected by the harbor police, he would be handed over to the executioner without delay. His plans had accordingly to be laid with the utmost caution.

One dark midnight, the fugitive crept out of a house in the garb of a servant. He carried a bundle and followed one of his friends, who walked in front with a dignified air wearing two swords, as if he were the master. By back streets and dark lanes, they found their way to the water's edge, where a small boat was already in waiting. Neesima climbed in the bottom of the boat and covered up with a tarpaulin as if he were a cargo of provisions. Then swiftly, but with muffled oars, the boatman pulled out to the schooner. A rope was thrown over the side, and the cargo, suddenly becoming very much alive, scrambled on board and hurried below. At last, the *Berlin* weighed anchor, spread her sails to an offshore breeze, and forged her way out to the open sea. Neesima now was safe and free. It was July 18, 1864, and the hero of our story was 21 years of age.

In Pursuit of a Great Aim

Neesima endured a very disagreeable passage to Shanghai and 10 days of wretchedness and uncertainty in that busy port, where he could not get rid of the idea that even yet he might be betrayed and sent back to Japan. Our adventurer then found another American vessel, the *Wild Rover*, bound for Boston, and succeeded in persuading the captain to take him on board without wages as his own personal servant. The voyage was a tedious one, for the *Wild Rover* sailed here and there about the China seas for eight months before turning homeward, and she spent four months more on the ocean passage.

In Hong Kong harbor, Neesima discovered a Chinese New Testament in a shop and felt that he must secure it at all costs. He had not a copper to his name, and having promised to work his passage without wages, felt that he could not ask the captain for any money. At last, he thought of his sword, which, being a samurai, he had brought with him as a matter of course. Could he honorably part with this weapon, which marked the dignity of his caste and was to him an indispensable badge of his own self-respect? He was not long in deciding. The Japanese sword was soon in the hands of a dealer and Neesima triumphantly bore his prize back to the ship. He read the book day and night and found in it answers to some of the questions which had so long perplexed his mind.

When the *Wild Rover* reached Boston, our hero's trials were by no means over. The Civil War had lately ended. Work was scarce; the price of everything was high. Nobody wanted this Japanese lad with his "pidgin" English and his demand to be sent to school. Neesima's first real comfort came from a copy of *Robinson Crusoe* which he picked up for a few cents in a secondhand bookstore. He was almost as friendless and solitary on the shores of this great continent as the shipwrecked mariner on that lonely island beach. But what appealed to Neesima most of all was Crusoe's prayers. Hitherto he had cried to God as an unknown God, feeling all the while that perhaps God had no eyes to see him and no ears to listen for him. Now he learned from Crusoe's manner of praying that in all his troubles he must cry to God as a present, personal friend. And so, day by day, in the full belief that God was listening, he uttered this prayer, "Please don't cast me away into miserable condition. Please let me reach my great aim."

Neesima's worst anxieties were nearly over now. His "great aim" was almost in sight. As soon as the *Wild Rover* reached Boston, the captain had gone off on a long visit to his friends, not thinking much about his Japanese cabin boy or expecting to see him again. But on his return to his ship some weeks after, he found "Joe," as the lad was called on shipboard, still hovering about the vessel as his one ark of refuge. This led him to speak to the ship's owner, Mr. Hardy, of the young man he had brought to America.

Mr. Hardy, who was a large-hearted and generous Christian man, at once declared that he would make some provision for the poor fellow. His first idea was to employ him as a house servant, but when his wife and he met the youth and heard his wonderful story, they saw immediately that this was no ordinary stowaway. Instead of making Neesima a servant, they took him into their family practically as an adopted son and gave him a thorough education, first in an academy at Andover and afterward at Amherst College.

It was in token of this adoption that, when he was baptized as a member of the Christian Church, he took his full name of Joseph Hardy Neesima. On shipboard, as has been mentioned, he was called Joe. The sailors decided that he must have some short and handy name, and Joe suggested itself as convenient. "Keep the name," Mr. Hardy said after hearing how it was given. For he felt that, like another Joseph who went down to Egypt as a captive and became the savior of his brethren, Joseph Neesima, the runaway samurai, might yet become a benefactor to his country. Mr. Hardy lived long enough to see his hopes realized.

FINDING A GREATER AIM

After graduating from Amherst College, Neesima entered himself as a student at Andover Theological Seminary with the view of being ordained as a fully qualified missionary to his own countrymen. Soon after this, a pathway for his return to Japan opened up in a dramatic manner.

Since Neesima's departure from Hakodate in 1864, the chariot wheels of progress had been moving rapidly in the land of his birth. A great political and social revolution had taken place. In pursuance of this new policy, there came to Washington in the winter of 1871-72 a distinguished delegation from the Imperial Court of Japan. It had for its special commission to inspect and report upon the workings of Western civilization. The delegation soon felt the need of someone who could not only act as interpreter, but also assist in the task of examining the institutions, and especially the educational institutions, of foreign lands.

For some time, Mr. Mori, the senior Japanese representative in the United States, had had his eye on his young countryman at Andover. He now invited Neesima to Washington to be introduced to the delegation. So favorable was the impression produced by his appearance, and so evident was it that he was thoroughly conversant with the principles and methods of Western culture, that he was immediately requested to accompany the ambassadors as an adviser on their tour through the United States and Europe. Overtures of the most flattering kind were made to Neesima, with brilliant prospects in the political world whenever he returned to his native land. But his mind was now fully made up regarding his work in life. When Neesima returned to Japan it would not be as a politician, but as a Christian missionary.

In the meantime, however, Neesima willingly put his services at the disposal of the Japanese delegation, and thereby not only greatly enlarged his experience, but gained influential friends among the rising statesmen of Japan. These friends were afterwards of no small help to him in his efforts to promote among his countrymen the cause of Christianity. The special task was assigned to Neesima of drawing up a paper on "The Universal Education of Japan." His essay became the basis of the report made by the embassy on the subject of education, and this report, with certain modifications, was the foundation of a new Japanese system of education.

After a year had been spent in this interesting way, Neesima returned to Andover. On the completion of his theological course, he was ordained by the American Board of Missions as an evangelist to his fellow countrymen. Ten years had now elapsed from the time when he was smuggled out of Japan in the hold of a little schooner as a poor and unknown lad and a criminal in the eyes of the law. He was about to return a highly cultured Christian gentleman with not a few influential friends on both sides of the Pacific. And he was returning with a purpose. He had found the light he came to seek, but he was far from being satisfied with that. His aim now was to be a light-bringer to Japan.

THE LIGHT-BRINGER

Neesima purposed to start a Christian college in which he could meet the craving of Young Japan for Western knowledge—the craving which he knew so well. At the same time, he planned to surround the students with a Christian atmosphere and train some of them to be preachers and teachers of Jesus Christ. He started his college, which he called the "Doshisha," or "Company of One Endeavour," not in any city of the coast, where Western ideas had become familiar, but in Kyoto, the sacred city of the interior. Kyoto was home to 6,000 temples and the very heart of the religious life of Old Japan.

In this place, where Buddhism and Shintoism had flourished unchallenged for a thousand years, Neesima was subjected for a time to the furious hatred of the traditional priests and even to the opposition of the magistrates. For the most part, these men had no objections to Western education, but Christian education they would have liked to suppress. It was now that Neesima realized the advantage of the friendship of the members of the delegation to the U.S. Several of those gentlemen had become prominent members of the Japanese Cabinet, and they did much to remove difficulties out of Neesima's way.

And so, the Doshisha took root and flourished. In the last year of its founder's life, when he had been engaged in his work for 15 years, the number of students in all departments, young women as well as young men, had risen to over 900. Neesima wore himself out by his labors and died in 1890 at the comparatively early age of 47.

The Doshisha is Neesima's living monument in Japan. By 1903, more than 5,000 students had passed through it, of whom above 80 were preachers of the gospel, 161 were teachers, 27 were government officials and 16 were newspaper editors. By turning out a succession of highly educated men and women, trained under Christian influences, Neesima's college has contributed no small part in the creation of that New Japan which swiftly stepped into the foremost rank of the great company of nations.

•••

Source Material. The chief authority for this chapter is *A Maker of New Japan: Joseph Hardy Neesima*, by Rev. J. D. Davis (New York: Fleming H. Revell Co., 1894).

PART VI

HEALING HANDS, BEAUTIFUL FEET

Jacob Chamberlain and George Mackay came from different countries and worked more than 2,500 miles apart, but they had a lot in common. Chamberlain was a medical doctor who pointed his patients toward the ultimate, heavenly source of the physical healing he provided. Mackay used dentistry to prove his goodwill and the power of the God he preached. Both men also traveled on foot over difficult terrain, bringing the truth of the gospel to people who had no other way of hearing of the good Creator God who loved them. Providing physical healing and relief opened the door to fruitful ministry for both Chamberlain and Mackay, and so opened the door for the Church to grow in some of the "ends of the earth" that Jesus spoke of before His ascension. That growth continues today, as faithful servants take the gospel to hard-to-reach places and hard-to-love people.

CHAPTER 11

SALVATION BY SCALPEL, STORY AND SNAKE

DR. JACOB CHAMBERLAIN IN INDIA

A WALKING AMBULANCE

THE COUNTRY OF THE TELUGUS stretched north-wards from Chennai[29] for some 500 miles along the shores of the Bay of Bengal, while to the west it extended about halfway across the peninsula. It was a region which attracted those who went to India for sport and adventure, for its jungles abounded in tigers and other wild animals. From the point of view of Christian missions, it had this special interest: that there was no part of all Hindustan[30] where the gospel was preached with more marked success or where the people gathered more rapidly into the Christian Church. One of the most enterprising missionaries in India was Dr. Jacob Chamberlain of the American Reformed Church.

On a typical morning, the doctor would be busy since sunrise with patients who came from far and near to be treated or prescribed for, until about 100 people gathered in front of the little dispensary. The heat of the day would now be coming on, but before dismissing them and distributing the medicines they had waited for, Dr. Chamberlain would take down his Telugu Bible,

---

29. A city on the southeast coast of India.
30. India.

read and explain a chapter, and then kneel to ask a blessing upon all who had need of healing.

It would now be breakfast time, and after several hours of hard work the doctor was always quite ready for a good meal. But one day, just as he was about to go home for that purpose, he heard the familiar chant used by the local people when carrying a heavy burden. Looking out, he saw four men approaching, two in front and two behind, with a long bamboo pole on their shoulders and a blanket slung on it in hammock fashion with a sick man inside. Behind this makeshift ambulance two men were walking, one leading the other by the hand.

In a few minutes, the sick man was laid in his blanket on the floor of the veranda and the little company told their tale. They had come from a village two days' journey off because they heard that the foreign doctor could work wonderful cures. The young man in the blanket was dying. The old man led by the hand was his uncle, who had recently grown blind. Their friends brought them to Dr. Chamberlain to see if he could make them well.

On examination, Dr. Chamberlain found that the young man's case was almost hopeless, but that there was just a chance of saving him by a serious surgical operation. This the doctor performed the same afternoon. At first, the patient seemed to be sinking under the shock, but he rallied by and by and gradually came back to health and strength again. The old man's blindness was a simpler case. An easy operation and careful treatment were all that were required. And so, when uncle and nephew had been in the hospital for a few weeks, the doctor was able to send them back to their village. The young man walked home on his own feet and the old man no longer needed to be led by the hand.

But here the story does not end. Every day while in the hospital the two patients had heard the doctor read a chapter from the Gospels and make its meaning plain. When the time for leaving came, they begged for a copy of the history of Jesus, "the Divine Guru," so that they might let all their neighbors know of the glad news they had heard. They acknowledged that they could not read, for they were poor weavers who had never been to school. "But when the cloth merchant comes to buy our fabric," they said, "we will gather the villagers and put the book into his hand and say, 'Read us this book, and then we will talk business.' And when the tax-gatherer comes we will say, 'Read us this book, and then we will settle our taxes.' Let us have the book, for we want all our village to know about the Divine Guru, Jesus Christ."

OFF WITH YOU AND GOOD RIDDANCE

The uncle and nephew got the book and went away, and for three years Dr. Chamberlain heard nothing of them. But at last, on a wide preaching tour, he met them again. They had learned of his approach, and when he entered the village at sunrise the whole population was gathered under the council tree. His two patients of three years ago came forward with smiling faces to greet him and told him that through the reading of the Bible everyone in the place had agreed to give up his idols if the doctor would send someone to teach them more about Jesus.

Dr. Chamberlain discussed the matter fully with them, and when he saw that they were thoroughly in earnest, promised to send a teacher as soon as possible. But just before leaving to proceed on his journey, he noticed, near at hand, the little village temple with its stone idols standing on their platform at the farther end of the shrine.

"What are you going to do with these idols now?" he said to the people.

"The idols are nothing to us any longer," they replied, "we have renounced them all."

"But are you going to leave them standing there in the very heart of the village?"

"What would you have us do with them?" they asked.

"Well," said the doctor, wishing to test their sincerity, "I would like to take one of them away with me." He knew the superstitious dread which even Indian believers are apt to entertain for the idols of their fathers and the unwillingness they usually have to lay violent hands on them. He did not expect anything more than that they might permit him to remove one of the images. But at this point the old man whose sight had been restored stepped forward and said, "I'll bring out the chief *swami* for you."

Going into the shrine, he shook the biggest idol from the plaster with which it was fastened to the stone platform and then

115

handed it to the doctor, saying as he did so something like this: "Well, old fellow, be off with you! We and our ancestors for a thousand years have feared and worshiped you. Now we have found a better God and are done with you. Be off with you, and a good riddance to us. Jesus is now our God and Savior."

And so, the ugly stone *swami* that had lorded it so long over the consciences of these Telugu villagers was "dethroned," as Dr. Chamberlain put it, "by the surgeon's knife." Jesus Christ, the Divine Guru, reigned in its stead.

JUDGING A BOOK BY ITS COVER

But now let us follow the doctor in some of the more striking episodes of one of his earliest tours. It was a journey of 1,200 miles through the kingdom of Hyderabad and on into Central India—a region where at that time no missionary had ever worked before. He rode all the way on a sturdy pony, accompanied by four Indian assistants with two cattle carts full of Gospels and other Christian literature which he hoped to sell to the people at low prices.

One of their first and most dangerous adventures was in the walled city of Hyderabad. They had already distributed a few Gospels and tracts when some Brahman priests and Muslim fanatics raised the mob against them. It was done in this way. A number of the Gospels were bound in cloth boards of a buff color. The Muslim zealots spread a rumor that these books were bound in pigskin—a thing which no true disciple of Muhammad will touch. The Brahmans, on the other hand, told their followers that these boards were made of calfskin—and to a Hindu, the cow is a sacred animal.

The crowd got thoroughly excited, and soon Dr. Chamberlain and his four helpers were standing in the marketplace with their backs to a wall while a howling multitude surged in front, many of whom had already begun to tear up the cobblestones with which the street was paved in order to stone the intruders to death.

The doctor saved the situation by getting permission to tell a wonderful story. The crowd's curiosity was aroused from the first, and soon their hearts were touched as they listened to a simple and graphic description of the death of Jesus on the cross. The stones dropped from the hands that clutched them, tears stood in many eyes and when the speaker had finished, every copy of the Gospels which had been brought into the city from the little camp outside the walls was eagerly bought up by priests as well as laypeople.

THE SERPENT-DESTROYER

Dangers of that sort were rare. For the most part, both in town and country, Dr. Chamberlain was welcomed courteously and gladly listened to as he stood in the busy marketplace or sat beside the village elders on the stone seat beneath the Council tree and explained the purpose of his coming. Dangers of another kind, however, were common enough. Once, when they were passing through the great teak forest, where the trees towered 150 feet above their heads, they came in sight of a large village in a forest clearing. As they drew near, the elders of the place came out to salute them. The doctor asked if they could give him a suitable place to pitch his tent. They did better than that, for they gave him the free use of a newly erected shed.

Somewhat tired out with a long forenoon's march, Dr. Chamberlain lay down to rest his limbs and took up his Greek Testament meanwhile to read a chapter. He held the book over his face as he lay stretched out on his back. By and by he let his arm fall, and suddenly became aware that a huge serpent was coiled on one of the bamboo rafters just above him. It had gradually been letting itself down until some four feet of its body was hanging directly over his head. Its tongue was already forked out—a sure sign that it was just about to strike. When studying the anatomy of the human frame, Dr. Chamberlain had sometimes wondered whether a person lying on his back could jump sideways without first erecting himself. He discovered on this occasion that, with a proper incentive, the thing could be done.

Bounding from his dangerous position, he ran to the door of the shed and took from the cattle cart which was standing there a huge iron spit five or six feet long, which was made for roasting meat in a jungle camp. With this as a spear he attacked the serpent and was successful at his first thrust in pinning it to the rafter round which it was coiled. Holding the spit firmly in its place to prevent the struggling animal from shaking it out, though he ran the utmost risk of being struck as it shot out its fanged mouth in its efforts to reach his hand, Dr. Chamberlain called loudly to his assistant to bring him a bamboo cane.

The Doctor in Peril

The cane was quickly brought, and then, still holding the spit in position with one hand, he beat the brute about the head till life was extinct. When quite sure that it was dead, he drew the spit out of the rafter and held it at arm's length on a level with his shoulder, the transfixed reptile hanging from it. He found that both the head and the tail touched the ground, thus showing that the serpent was not less than 10 feet long.

Just at that moment, the village watchman looked in at the door and then passed on quickly into the village. Immediately it flashed into the doctor's mind that he had got himself into trouble, for he remembered that these people worshiped serpents as gods. They never dared to kill one, and if they saw a stranger trying to do so, would intercede for its life.

Dr. Chamberlain was still considering what to do when he saw the chief men of the village advancing. To his surprise, they were carrying brass trays covered with sweetmeats, coconuts and limes. His surprise was greater still when, as they reached the doorway in which he stood to meet them, they bowed down before him to the ground and presented their simple offerings, hailing him at the same time as the deliverer of their village.

That deadly serpent, they told him, had been the terror of the place for several years. It had killed a child and several of their cattle. They had never ventured to attack it, for they knew that if any of them did so he would be accursed. The kindred of the dead serpent would wage war upon that man and his family until every one of them was exterminated. But Dr. Chamberlain, a visitor, had killed it without their knowledge or consent. They were freed from the pest of their lives, and at the same time were absolutely guiltless of its blood.

Their gratitude knew no bounds. The villagers pressed upon the doctor the fattest sheep in their flocks. They sent the village crier with his tom-tom all around the place to summon the people to come and hear the words of "the serpent-destroyer." And when Dr. Chamberlain seized the opportunity to speak to them about "that old serpent called the devil" and One who came to bruise the serpent's head, they listened to him as he had rarely been listened to before.

•••

Source Material. The material for this chapter is derived from Dr. Chamberlain's two books, *In the Tiger Jungle* and *The Cobra's Den* (New York: Fleming H. Revell Co., 1896 and 1900).

CHAPTER 12

PULLING TEETH, PLANTING CHURCHES

GEORGE MACKAY IN TAIWAN

FORCEPS AND A BIBLE

THE ACQUAINTANCE OF Dr. George Leslie Mackay with Formosa[31] and its people—the people of the mountains as well as of the plains—is of an altogether unique kind. The young Canadian of Highland Scottish descent was sent out to China as a missionary by the Presbyterian Church of Canada. He was given a free hand in the selection of a definite sphere and chose the northern part of Formosa—perfectly virgin soil so far as any Christian work was concerned.

Formosa was a wild and lawless land with a mixture of mutually hostile people, men of the plains and men of the mountains, corrupt officials in the towns and violent headhunters in the hill forests. Mackay, however, went about fearlessly with a dentist's forceps in one hand and a Bible in the other. At times, he slept contentedly in the filthy cabin of a farmer on the swampy rice plains with a litter of pigs for his bedfellows (the pig being a highly domesticated animal in Formosa and treated by its master as an Englishman treats his pet dog). At other times, he ventured far up among the mountains in the land of

---

31. Taiwan.

the headhunters, where his sleeping apartment, which was also the sleeping apartment of the whole family, was adorned with a row of grinning skulls that testified to the prowess of his host in murdering the dwellers on the plains. It was by a courage and persistence which nothing could daunt that this young Scoto-Canadian won his way in Formosa.

A LAND OF MUTUAL HOSTILITY

The population of Formosa was divided between the indigenous peoples, who were of Malayan descent, and the Chinese, who in ever-increasing numbers poured in from the adjacent mainland. Though only half the size of Scotland, the island is dominated by a range of mountains quite Alpine in their height, the loftiest rising to between 14,000 and 15,000 feet above the sea. Along the coast, however, there are fertile stretches, perfectly flat, formed by the alluvial deposits washed down in the course of ages. On the richer of these plains, as well as on the lower reaches of the hills, the incoming Chinese settled, usually by no better title than the right of might.

To the Chinese, of course, the original inhabitants without exception were "barbarians," but the Malayan population, though comprising a great many different tribes, may be roughly divided into two well-defined sections. First, there were those who had accepted Chinese authority, and in a modified form had adopted the Chinese civilization and religion. These went by the name of Pe-po-hoan, or "barbarians of the plain." Then there were those who had absolutely refused to acknowledge the Chinese invaders as the masters of Formosa and, though driven into the mountains and forests, retained their ancestral freedom. These were the much-dreaded Chhi-hoan or "raw barbarians." Among these mountain peoples, headhunting is cultivated as a fine art. They hated the Chinese with a deadly hatred, and hardly less their own Pe-po-hoan kinsfolk who had yielded to the stranger and accepted his ways. Pe-po-hoan and Chinese skulls were mingled indiscriminately in their ghastly collections, which were the chief glory of the mountain braves, as they formed the principal adornment of their dwellings.

MAKING DISCIPLES...

Naturally it was among the Chinese in the towns that Mackay began his work. He was fortunate in gathering round him very early some earnest young men who not only accepted Christianity for themselves but became his disciples and followers with a view to teaching and helping others. These students, as they were called, accompanied him on all his tours, not only gaining valuable experience thereby, but being of real assistance in various ways.

Dentistry and the Gospel

For instance, Mackay soon discovered that the people of Formosa, partly because of the prevalence of malarial fever and partly because they were constantly chewing the betel nut, had very rotten teeth and suffered dreadfully from toothache. Though not a doctor, he knew a little of medicine and surgery, having attended classes in these subjects by way of preparing himself for his work abroad. He found that nothing helped him so much in making his way among the people as his modest skill in dentistry.

The priests and other enemies of Christianity might persuade the people that their fevers and other ailments had been cured, not by the medicines of the "foreign devil," but by the intervention of their own gods. The power of the missionary, however, to give instantaneous relief to one in the agonies of toothache was unmistakable, and tooth extraction worked wonders in breaking down prejudice and opposition. It was here that some of the students proved especially useful. They also learned to draw teeth so that, between them, they were able to treat as many as 500 patients in an afternoon.

The usual custom of Mackay and his little band of disciples as they journeyed about the country was to take their stand in an open space, often on the stone steps of a temple. After singing a hymn or two to attract attention, they proceeded to the work of tooth-pulling. Then they invited the people to listen to their message. For the most part, the crowd was very willing to listen. Sudden relief from pain produces gratitude even toward a "foreign devil," and the suspicion of some black arts or other evil designs was always guarded against by scrupulously placing the tooth of each patient in the palm of his own hand. The people began to love Mackay, and this opened their hearts to his preaching. Men and women came to confess their faith and in one large village, which was the center of operations, there were so many converts that a preaching hall had to be secured. Sunday after Sunday, it was packed by an expectant crowd.

Opposition is often the best proof of success, and in Mackay's case it soon came in cruel and tragic forms. A cunning plot was laid between the priestly party and the civil officials to accuse a number of these Chinese Christians of conspiring to assassinate the mandarin. Six innocent men were seized and put in stocks in the dungeons of the city of Bang-kah.[32] Mock trials were held, in the course of which the prisoners were bambooed, made to kneel on red-hot chains and tortured in various other ways. At last, one morning, two of the heroic band, a father and son, were taken out of the dungeon and dragged off to the place of execution. The son's head was chopped off before his father's eyes, after which the old man, too, was put to death. Their heads were fastened above the city gate for a terror and a warning to all who passed by. It was a cruel fate, and yet better than that of the remaining prisoners. Their lot was to be slowly starved or tortured to death in filthy dungeons.

But in spite of these horrors—partly, we might say, because of

---

32. Now a district of Taipei.

them—the number of Christians in North Formosa steadily grew until at length, as Dr. Mackay puts it, "Bang-kah itself was taken." Not that this important place was transformed into a Christian city. But it ceased, at all events, to be fiercely anti-Christian and came to honor the very man whom it had hustled, hooted at, pelted with mud and rotten eggs and often plotted to kill.

A striking proof of the change was given by and by when Mackay was about to return to Canada on a visit. The head men of the city sent a delegation to ask him to allow them to show their appreciation of himself and his work by according him a public sendoff. Mackay was not sure about it at first, not caring much for demonstrations of this kind. But on reflection he concluded that it might do good to the Christian cause to allow the head men to have their own way. So he was carried through the streets of Bang-kah to the jetty in a silk-lined sedan chair, preceded by the officials of the place and followed by 300 soldiers and bands of civilians bearing flags and banners. Musical accompaniment was provided by no fewer than eight Chinese orchestras made up of cymbals, drums, gongs, pipes, guitars, mandolins, tambourines and clarinets.

...WHO MAKE DISCIPLES

But while Mackay found his base of operations among the Chinese in the north and west of Formosa, he did not forget the Malayan tribes, whether those of the plains or those of the mountains. As soon as he had got a firm footing and gathered a band of competent disciples around him, he began to turn his attention to the Pe-po-hoan, the "barbarians of the plain." They cultivated their rice farms in the low-lying and malarial districts along the northeast coast.

The Pe-po-hoan did not prove at first a friendly or receptive people. From village after village, Mackay and his companions were turned away with reviling, the inhabitants often setting their wolfish dogs upon them. The weather was bad, and in that low-lying region the roads were soon turned into quagmires where their feet sank into 18 inches of mud. When night fell, sometimes no better sleeping place could be had than the lee side of a dripping rice stack.

After a while, things began to improve. Like Jesus in Galilee, Mackay found his first disciples in the Kap-tsu-lan plain among the fishermen—bold, hardy fellows who lived in scattered villages along that coast. Three of these fishermen came to him one day and said, "You have been going through and through our plain, and no one has received you. Come to our village, and we will listen to you."

They led Mackay and his Chinese disciples to their village and gave them a good supper of rice and fish. Then one of them took a large conch shell, which in other days had served as a war trumpet, and summoned the whole population to an assembly. Till the small hours of the morning, Mackay was kept busy preaching, conversing, discussing and answering questions. The very next day, these people determined to have a church of their own in which to worship the true God. Bricks were made out of mud and rice chaff and a primitive little chapel was soon erected in which every evening, at the blowing of the conch, the entire village met to hear the preacher.

Mackay stayed two months in this place, and by that time it had become nominally Christian. Several times he dried his dripping clothes at night in front of a fire made of idolatrous paper, idols and ancestral tablets which the people had given him to destroy. One reason for this rapid and wholesale conversion to Christianity no doubt lay in the fact that the Chinese idolatry which these Pe-po-hoan fishermen had been induced to accept never came very near to their hearts. Originally, they or their fathers had been nature-worshipers, and many of them were inclined to look upon the rites and ceremonies to which they submitted as unwelcome reminders of their subjection to outsiders.

What took place in this one village was soon repeated in several others on the Kap-tsu-lan plain. By and by, no fewer than 19 chapels sprang up in that plain, the preachers and pastors in every case being from Formosa, and several of them being drawn from among the Pe-po-hoan themselves.

CHRISTMAS IS FOR CANNIBALS, TOO

But something must now be said about the Chhi-hoan, or "barbarians of the mountains." One who traveled among such people literally took his life in his hands, for he might at any moment have fallen victim to treachery or to passion for human blood. But perfect courage and unvarying truth and kindness will carry a traveler far, and Mackay had the further advantage of being possessed of medical and surgical skill. And so, by degrees, Mackay came to live in close touch with the Chhi-hoan.

Chhi-hoan Hunters

One year, Mackay spent a Christmas holiday high up among the mountains as the guest of one of the Chhi-hoan chiefs. The house was a single large room, fully 30 feet long, in which at night a fire blazed at either end. Around one fire the women squatted, spinning cord for nets. Around the other the braves smoked and discussed a headhunting expedition which they proposed to undertake before long. On the walls were the customary rows of skulls, their grinning teeth lighted up fitfully by the flickering gleams from the burning fire logs.

But before the time came to lie down and rest, Mackay proposed that he and his Christian companions should give a song, a proposal which secured silence at once, for the Chhi-hoan are very fond of singing. And so, on Christmas night, in that wild spot where no white man had ever been before, and to that strange audience, Mackay and his little band of Chinese disciples sang some Christian hymns. And after that, he told the story of the first Christmas night and of the love of Him who was born in the stable at Bethlehem, no less for the headhunters of Formosa than for the white men whose home was over the sea.

•••

Source Material. The material for this chapter is derived from Dr. Mackay's *From Far Formosa* (Edinburgh: Oliphant, Anderson, & Ferrier, 1896).

WHY READ OLD BOOKS?

I N 1944, LESS THAN 40 years after John Lambert wrote *The Romance of Missionary Heroism*, C.S. Lewis penned an introduction to a new translation of the 4th century masterpiece *On the Incarnation* by Athanasius. In that introduction, a masterpiece in its own right, Lewis addresses the question of why we should bother to read old books when there are so many new ones. He writes, "There is a strange idea abroad that in every subject the ancient books should be read only by the professionals, and that the amateur should content himself with the modern books." Lewis was writing primarily about theological and philosophical literature, but the same perception persists about the biographies of missionaries of centuries past. We imagine thick books entombed in the basements of missiological libraries, layered in dust and encoded with old fonts and weird spelling, inviting us to admire them, but not necessarily to read them. Instead, we content ourselves with an occasional inspirational quote or sermon illustration extracted for us (by professionals) from the writings of or about well-known missionaries.

Lewis explains that "The error [of avoiding old books] is rather an amiable one, for it springs from humility," but in the case of biographies, humility is not always our hang-up. Sometimes we avoid them because they are long, dense and intimidating, but sometimes we shudder at vocabulary and ideas that strike us as insensitive or ethnocentric. This text clears up most of those issues as a modern adaptation, but what if you pick up Lambert's 1907 original or one of the biographies it is based on? Are the old books of missionary sacrifice and adventure still worth reading if they contain stereotypes or smack of colonialism? Why does it matter what James Gilmour or Mary Calvert did in the 1800s? Why not just read newsletters from living, breathing missionaries who wear jeans and talk about "sharing truth with the unreached" instead of "converting the uncivilized barbarians?"

If you want C.S. Lewis's advice (and why wouldn't you?), beware that as "an amateur" you are "much less protected than the expert against the dangers of an exclusive contemporary diet." Some modern books are wonderful, but it is too soon to tell which ones. As Lewis explains, "A new book is still on its trial and the amateur is not in a position to judge it. It has to be tested against the great body of Christian thought down the ages, and all its hidden implications (often unsuspected by the author himself) have to be brought to light." We can't be sure for another hundred years which of the missionary biographies being written today are worth passing down through the generations. The old books have already proven themselves, particularly the ones that continue to be updated, anthologized and reprinted. Lewis suggests that we divide our reading time between the old and the new. *Fire and Ice* stands on middle ground as a modern adaptation of an old book, much like the translation of *On the Incarnation* that Lewis was introducing.

Lewis offers a second argument in favor of old books: "Every age has its own outlook. It is specially good at seeing certain truths and specially liable to make certain mistakes. We all, therefore, need the books that will correct the characteristic mistakes of our own period. And that means the old books." In essence, don't read biographies of old missionaries because they were *better* than us. Read them because they were *different* than us, and that means we can learn from them. Lewis denies that there is "any magic about the past. People were no cleverer then than they are now; they made as many mistakes as we. But not the same mistakes."

When the errors, sins, ignorance and anachronisms of past generations of missionaries leap out at you from the pages of an old book, don't throw away the book. Their faults aren't going to hurt you. You see things that they didn't. Keep reading to find out what they saw that you haven't yet. In Lewis's words, "They will not flatter us in the errors we are already committing; and their own errors, being now open and palpable, will not endanger us. Two heads are better than one, not because either is infallible, but because they are unlikely to go wrong in the same direction." You won't want to adopt all of the mindsets or mimic all of the methodologies of missionaries of past centuries, but you probably won't want to sign up for all of their sacrifices or endure all of their suffering either.

A third reason to read old books in general, and missionary biographies in particular, is that they reveal the essential unity of the faith (in general) and the global redemption narrative (in particular) that have motivated Christians to seek out the ends of the earth for thousands of years. Our world is changing at a disorienting pace, but that does not mean that everything has changed. Our Great Commission task of making obedient disciples of all the peoples of the world is not subject to shifting political, economic, social or any other category of forces that can, at times, feel like they threaten and divide us.

Christianity, the Church, missions—they can feel scattered and fractured. "But," Lewis cautions, "if any man is tempted to think—as one might be tempted who read only contemporaries—that 'Christianity' is a word of so many meanings that it means nothing at all, he can learn beyond all doubt, by stepping out of his own century, that this is not so." Unity and division are a matter of perspective. "We are all rightly distressed," Lewis admits, "and ashamed also, at the divisions of Christendom. But those who have always lived within the Christian fold may be too easily dispirited by them...Seen from [the outside], what is left intact despite all the divisions, still appears (as it truly is) an immensely formidable unity."

Missionaries today serve the same God for the same reasons Joseph Neesima and Jacob Chamberlain did in the 1800s. Our methods must adapt to our circumstances, but we are united with those who went before us, the "great cloud of witnesses" who surround us (Hebrews 12:1). Some of those witnesses wrote books, and with a little effort you can track them down on the internet or in a library. Dusty covers and weird fonts or not, you'll discover in them the unity that Lewis claims any of us can find "by going out of his own age."

To sum up, read missionary biographies because they are proven, because they reveal our mistakes without threatening us with theirs and because they mark the continuity in the spread of the gospel across the world and across the centuries. We hope, as

Lambert did, that reading the stories of *Fire and Ice* will motivate you to seek out other collections, anthologies and biographies of missionary heroes. And we hope that the old stories "suggest to some who are looking forward to the future with a high ambition, and wondering how to make the most of life, whether there is any career which offers so many opportunities of romantic experience and heroic achievement as that of a Christian missionary."[33]

---

33. From Lambert's introduction to *The Romance of Missionary Heroism*, 1907.